Common Sense for a World of Common Nonsense

Donald DeMarco

En Route Books and Media, LLC
St. Louis, MO
USA

… **ENROUTE**
Make the time

En Route Books and Media, LLC
5705 Rhodes Avenue
St. Louis, MO 63109

Cover credit: Sebastian Mahfood using Dalle-E

Copyright © 2025 Donald DeMarco

ISBN-13: 979-8-88870-370-0

Library of Congress Control Number: 2025939256

No part of this book may be reproduced, stored in a retrieval system, or transmitted in any form, or by any means, electronic, mechanical, photocopying, or otherwise, without the prior written permission of the author.

Dedication

This book is gratefully dedicated to James Ridley and Sebastian Mahfood, two publishers who understand the supreme value of the Word. January 29, 2025.

The author wishes to thank Tom, Kristen, Paul, Anne, Peggy, James, and Sebastian for their help and inspiration.

Epigraphs

"In the past, and even to this day, there have been so many programs promising 'healing' for the world and proclaiming the arrival of 'true' justice in men's dealings with one another. But none of these can be regarded as complete unless it is linked with the justification before God—which is the main foundation of all justice . . . Saint John Paul II, *Sign of Contradiction*

"Since the modern world began in the sixteenth century, nobody's system of philosophy has really corresponded to everybody's sense of reality; to what, if left to themselves, common men would call common sense." . . . . G. K. Chesterton

"We recommend avoiding general and often dehumanizing 'the' labels such as the poor, the mentally ill, the French, the disabled, the college-educated." . . . . . . Associated Press Stylebook

Synopsis

The great advantage that nonsense has over common sense is that it is unlimited. One can be nonsensical without boundaries. He can enjoy a freedom that escapes the shackles of reason. Common sense, on the other hand, is reined in by reality. It may seem unadventurous, but it forms the irreplaceable basis for all our adventures. "Common sense," in the words of Ralph Waldo Emerson, "is genius in its working clothes." It is, we may add, the basis for science and a pre-requisite for a sense of humor. We need common sense to build bridges and to laugh at common nonsense. Furthermore, "Common sense to an uncommon degree," as Samuel Taylor Coleridge maintains, "is what the world calls wisdom." Or, as playwright and novelist William Inge puts it, "The wisdom of the wise is an uncommon degree of common sense."

The question of the day, however, is whether common nonsense has overtaken common sense. Author and neurosurgeon Dr. Ben Carson, who was a presidential candidate in 2016, laments that, "People all over the nation are starved for honesty and common sense." Common sense has now become little more than an object of nostalgia. Has common sense reached its point of expiration?

It was not long ago when the following statements were held firmly in the embrace of common sense: That marriage is a union between a man and a woman; that the best arrangement for a child is to have a mother and father; that we have something to learn from tradition; that virtue is more powerful than vice; that prejudice is a sin against justice; that the Golden Rule is a sound ethical principle; that truth has an important place in a sound education; that philosophy can be illuminating; that we cannot live without hope in God; and that humility should be self-evident. These bromides have not only been brought into question, but also turned upside down.

The turmoil that is the offspring of the woke ideology along with diversity, inclusivity, and equity attests to the sheer nonsense involved in trying to put a square peg into a round hole. Advancing from common sense to common nonsense is not progress. Nor is it a bold adventure. It is an impractical dream, a failure, a farce, and a fiasco.

Synopsis

This book is an appeal for the restitution of common sense. At the same time, it exposes how deviations from common sense, like a train going off the tracks, can lead to ruin. Common sense is our starting point. Society cannot advance unless it begins at the beginning.

Waterloo, Ontario, September 15, 2004

Part One

Common Nonsense

I

Ideology vs. Reality

Is an Ideology Stronger than a Reality?

Duke Law has cited some interesting statistics in an article by Dorianne Lambelet Coleman and Wickliffe Shreve entitled "Comparing Athletic Performances: The Best Elite Women to Boys and Men." They offer two rather compelling examples to illustrate male superiority in athletic events."

Tori Bowie was considered the fastest woman in the world. Her career highlights include a 100-meter world championship (in the woman's category), and three Olympic medals, one of which is gold. Her best time in the 100-meter event, in 2017, was 10.78 seconds. That record, within the same year, was bettered by men and boys 15,000 (fifteen thousand) times.

Similarly, U. S. Champion Allyson Felix's 400 meters lifetime best was 40.26 seconds. That record, also in 2017, was bettered, again, by 15,000 men and boys throughout the world.

Overall, the authors state, there is an average 10-12% performance gap between elite males and elite females. The gap is smaller between elite females and non-elite males, but it's still "insurmountable."

These statistics offer a definitive justification for segregating sporting events for men and woman, something that been done consistently throughout the world and from the first Olympiad in 776 B. C.

These statistics cannot be refuted. But they can be pushed aside and replaced by wholly unrealistic ideologies such as diversity and inclusivity. Fatima Goss Graves is the president of the National Women's Law Center. Appearing before the House Oversight Committee on transgender competitors in female sports, she stated that female athletes should learn to lose gracefully to biological men. This is not the message that female cyclists want to hear after transgender males stole first and second place in the Illinois women's championship race. They would like their competitions to be what they claim to be, namely for female participants only.

Ms. Graves downplayed the male's inherent advantages over female athletes because "body diversity is an inherent part of sports." She rejected tests to verify athletes who claim to be female because they "inherently cause harm because of their invasive and traumatizing nature." The tests would reveal something that President Graves does not want to know, the real biological nature of a particular athlete. She stated that excluding trans women (biological males) hurts all women. Real women disagree. "Inclusivity," by excluding many women from winning athletic events, can deprive them of professional or academic opportunities.

On April 19, 2024, the Biden administration published changes to Title IX to include "gender identity." The changes, predictably, will create a backlash since nearly half the states have passed laws protecting women and men from the transgender ideology which manifests itself in sports, sex-exclusive locker rooms, and restrooms. Schools that fail to follow these rules would be subject to investigations and risk losing federal funding.

Julianne Young, a member of the Idaho's legislature who introduced the State's Definition of Sex law, which affirms that there are only two sexes, male and female, expressed her outrage that the Biden's administration abuses a law originally designed to protect women now places them in danger. "It is outrageous," she said, "and unconscionable that the Biden administration is now using civil rights law to protect women to assault them, undermining their privacy, dignity and safety."

According to the new changes, barring a transgendered athlete from competing in a female sporting event will be considered discriminatory. It gives the word "discriminate" a wider application than is reasonable. It allows, in effect, the fox to enter the chicken coup. Contrary to the reasonable preferences of women and girls, a trans woman (biological male) can enter their designated washrooms. Former secretary of Education told the *Washington Examiner* that Biden's changes "may well be the most anti-woman regulation of all time."

Gender ideology is based on the notion that a person's sex has nothing to do with biology and everything to do with how he feels. Historically, this type of confusion would be a sign of serious mental confusion and treated accordingly. Today, now that it is being enshrined in law, it requires compliance. The new democracy requires that all of us should be crazy.

Philosophy is concerned with reality. Politics, like advertising, is concerned with pleasing everybody, an impossible task. Law, being an ordinance of reason, should be on the side of philosophy. At present, law is bending toward politics in the worse sense and becoming an ordinance of unreason.

When Biden was elected president of the United States, his stated goal was to unify the country and avoid extremism. He has done exactly the opposite, dividing the country more than it has been since the Civil War, and supporting the LGBT+ consortium while appointing members of the far left. In addition, when he took office, he swore in the Bible to uphold and defend the Constitution. And yet, he urgently desires a new Constitution and has stated that it is "outrageous" that it does not provide a right to abortion. As Tom Shakely, Chief Engagement Officer at Americans United for Life, has remarked, "Our new elites swear an oath to uphold and defend the U. S. Constitution, yet strangely lack consensus on the nature of that document."

The Biden Administration presumes that an ideology is placed on firmer ground than a reality. It believes that something that does not exists is superior to something that does exist. Reality may be surprising or even terrifying, but it is the only basis that works. G. K. Chesterton has the right order of things and expresses it with a touch of humor: "It is one thing to describe an interview with a gorgon or a griffin, a creature who does not exist. It is another thing to discover that the rhinoceros does exist and then take pleasure in the fact that he looks as if he didn't." Elsewhere, he writes: "Truth, of course, must of necessity be stranger than fiction, for we have made fiction to suit ourselves."

The Death of Motherhood

The primary focus of the abortion debate is the nature and significance of the fetus. Is it human, does it have rights, or is it something less than human that can be dispatched at will? But there is a second focus of the debate, and that has to do with the nature and meaning of motherhood. The abortion issue is also a battleground for the nature and meaning of motherhood. Does motherhood, in its essence, include the right to induced abortion?

In addition to abortion, technological interventions such as artificial insemination, surrogate motherhood, embryo transfer, and *in vitro* fertilization have intensified the question concerning the nature and meaning of motherhood. The traditional presumption that a mother is the person from whom the child emerges is no longer universally accepted. There may be as many as four women at the same time vying for the title of mother: the one who conceives, the one who gestates, the one who delivers, and the one who rears the child.

The problem of motherhood becomes even more exacerbated in the light of gender-change ideology. The argument is made that a man can become a mother. In this regard, motherhood becomes politicized. The fact that more and more people are protesting the continuance of Mother's Day is a strong indication that motherhood is losing its hallowed status.

It is now possible for a woman to avoid marriage, intercourse, conception, and gestation and still be called a mother. This is possible because of IVF in combination with surrogate gestation. At the same time, it is possible for a woman to be married, conceive, gestate, and deliver a child and not be called a mother. This is possible because of surrogate motherhood. The question of who is the mother in particular cases has been adjudicated in the courts. The nature of motherhood, in some situations, has been left to the discretion of judges, lawyers, or surrogate brokers.

The politics of abortion adds further complications. Supreme Court Justice Ruth Bader Ginsburg, has declared that a woman who is pregnant but planning to have an abortion is not a mother. But if she is not called a "mother," is the omission of the term consistent with the original meaning of motherhood? Is it also inconsistent with the original notion of motherhood that a pregnant woman could willingly abort her child?

The great question is whether motherhood is something sacred? If it is, then it is inviolable. Any manipulation or distortion to accommodate extrinsic interests would therefore be sacrilegious. The present culture has, to a large extent, lost sight of the sacred in general. Blasphemy is common. Religion is scoffed. Even the Holy Mass is not immune from ridicule. Historian James Hitchcock wrote *The Recovery of the Sacred* to address the fact that honoring what is sacred was slipping away within the Catholic Church. Motherhood, to a certain extent, is no longer venerated; it is manipulated.

Mary, the mother of God, is the archetype of motherhood. She freely conceived her child, carried Him to term, and delivered Him. And she cared for Him as a mother cares for her child. There is no bifurcation or compromise in her maternity.

Theologian Raniero Cantalamessa, in his book *Mary: Mirror of the Church*, speaks of two types of unfulfilled maternities. One is abortion in which the child is conceived but not born. The other in which the child is born, but whose life began in a Petri dish, is not conceived in the mother's body. He contrasts these two types with Mary, the mother of God, who conceived Jesus and gave birth to Him. These two events are accorded feast days: the Annunciation and the Nativity. Mary defines motherhood as both fulfilled and undefiled. Pope Saint Paul VI conferred upon Mary the title "Mother of the Church," indicating the breadth of her motherhood. It is this understanding of motherhood that has died in the mind of the present culture. Today, a woman can choose the type of motherhood that corresponds to her situation. The more technology is involved in changing the meaning of motherhood, the more motherhood loses its sacred quality and becomes merely a choice.

The integrity of motherhood is essential to the integrity of the family. That integrity rests on the integrity of marriage, which, in turn, rests on respect for the special meaning of sexual union. Popular books for children, such as *Heather Has Two Mommies* and *Two Moms, the Zark & Me,* blatantly disregard the integrity of the family that is based on the singularity of motherhood. They promote new family forms that function apart for any regard for the sanctity of motherhood.

When motherhood is properly respected, it has a most beneficial effect on family members, but also those outside the family. With the dignity of motherhood in mind, people who are single realize more acutely that sexual intimacy can confer motherhood on a woman. Hence, they must take such intimacy with great seriousness, for motherhood, sacred as it is, is hard work, carrying immense responsibilities, and demanding great love. Considering the wholeness of motherhood, shining like a beacon, sexual intimacy is placed in a larger and more realistic perspective.

Motherhood is spiritual as well as biological. It is precisely in her spirituality that a mother extends her care both to her immediate family and to the world. Society loses an important modality of care when motherhood is compromised. Motherhood casts her salutary rays best when it is honored in its sacredness.

Is Guilt Peculiarly Christian?

A student once said to me, with an air of confidence that was wholly unjustified, that we would have a far better world if there were no guilt. He was assuming that guilt is some kind of artificial quirk that prevented people from being happy. Well, to give the devil his due, he was, without realizing it, half right.

Guilt is the recognition of one's complicity in wrongdoing. Francis Braceland, M. D., and Michael Stock, M. D., remark in their study *Modern Psychiatry: a Handbook for Believers* that "guilt is an objective state, existing when the individual has broken a law or moral imperative." Since the world has suffered from a great deal of wrongdoing, guilt is very real. Now, if there were not a single instance of wrongdoing (sin in the Christian vocabulary), there would be no basis for guilt. This is highly unlikely to happen, however, even though moralists from the beginning of culture have strongly and sternly warned against wrongdoing. On the other hand, to commit wrongful acts—larceny, assault, adultery, blasphemy, murder—without feeling any sense of guilt is pathological. Our world would most assuredly not be better off if it were replete with pathological characters.

My student would have been on safer ground if he had said that the world would be far better if more people sought forgiveness for their sins. In this instance, he would have been acknowledging both the reality of guilt and how it can be expiated. If Christians throughout the ages have been accused of being scrupulous, it is simply because, in their desire to be better human beings, they are acutely aware of their sins.

History makes it abundantly clear that guilt is not, by any means, peculiarly Christian. Guilt was fully recognized before Christianity came into being and in countries that are not Christian. Anna Elizabeth Wilhelm-Hooijbergh has published the fruit of her research in a book entitled *Peccatum: sin and guilt in ancient Rome.* The Old Testament fully acknowledges the reality of guilt. The same can be said for books that provide the moral basis for other religions.

The reality of wrongdoing (or criminal acts) is definitively established by the courts since the pursuit of justice would not be possible without making the crucial distinction between "guilty" and "not guilty." The recognition of sin and its expiation through forgiveness are universally acknowledged.

It is to Christianity's credit that it fully recognizes sin, guilt, and forgiveness. The same cannot be said of the secular world. The world remembers but does not forgive. "To err is human, to forgive is against departmental policy," reads a sign posted at the Los Angeles Police Department. Richard Nixon will never be forgiven for the Watergate fiasco. The obituary for Fred Snodgrass, who had a successful career as both a major league baseball player and as a businessman, reads as follows, "Fred Snodgrass, whose muff of a fly ball cost the New York Giants the 1912 World Series . . . " Lawyers do not forgive; they prosecute. Errors in baseball are recorded for posterity, but never erased.

To err is human, but to forgive is divine. Hence the importance of the Christian religion. It is able to do what the world cannot do. It can remove guilt by expiating guilt. Erich Fromm, who is not a Christian, points out in his book *The Sane Society* that "All figures show that Protestant countries have a much higher suicide rate than Catholic countries and suggests that the one explanation for this is the more adequate means to deal with a sense of guilt by the Catholic Church." Father Alfred Wilson, C. P., states in his book *Pardon and Peace* that modern psychologists have found from practical experience that many nervous breakdowns can be traced to a sense of guilt from unconfided and unforgiven sins. He remarks that Sigmund Freud admitted that, among his cases of serious psychological disorders, he never had a genuinely practicing Catholic.

Catholic poet and essayist Phyllis McGinleym, in her Introduction to the Time edition of C. S. Lewis' *Screwtape Letters*, states that "of all losses man has sustained in the past hundred years, no deprivation has been so terrible as the abandonment of guilt." Interpreting sin as a *faux pas*, an indiscretion, an embarrassment, has rendered man ineligible for the forgiveness that allows a person to return to wholeness. It is well known that repressed guilt can cause serious levels of anxiety.

Genuine sin, that is, real sin, is often confused with false sin. False, or neurotic, guilt may result from a person's being scrupulous, or failing to live up to certain social values that are entirely arbitrary. Psychiatrists help patients to distinguish sins that need to be forgiven from the mere feeling of guilt that does not require forgiveness. Paul Tournier has distinguished true from false guilt in terms of the former having its source in an opposition to God, while the latter originates in an opposition to the laws of men.

Guilt is not peculiarly Christian. It is universal. The Catholic Church, however, has been and continues to be, best prepared to acknowledge guilt and provide a remedy for it in the form of forgiveness. By sinning, one strays from reality as well as from himself. The expiation of guilt provides a certain freedom for the penitent which allows him to return to reality and, at the same time, to his better self. Breaking a mirror is not a sin, nor does it bring bad luck. Knocking on wood or throwing salt over one's left shoulder does not expiate guilt.

Can a Politician Afford to Tell the Truth?

The typical politician is a strange animal. He wants everyone's votes and therefore attempts to please everyone. He is not discouraged by the universal and unbreakable law that "you can't please everyone." Nonetheless, he resorts to a rhetoric that sparkles on the outside but fizzles on the inside. He may hold office, but not for long. His thin rhetoric burns out very quickly.

Donald Trump, for example, predicts that "everybody will like me" for presenting a view on abortion that will please everyone. This, of course, is like searching for the goose that lays the golden egg, or finding a pot of gold at the end of the rainbow. Abortion brooks no compromise. Since life begins at conception, being pro-life means opposing abortion at any stage of development. Being pro-choice means choosing whether or not to have an abortion. The two sides are irreconcilable. Nonetheless, promising a consensus creates the impression that one has hit upon a formula that will please everyone. But an impression is like a soap bubble. It is interesting while it lasts, but it does not last very long. Trump might as well say, "I am neither pro-life nor pro-choice. But vote for me anyway."

Nikki Haley asks pro-choicers to respect her pro-life views as she respects theirs. This may sound magnanimous, but it is quite meaningless. Respect must be earned. Not every position is worthy of respect. Are views of Nazis, members of the Taliban, Isis, or Al-Qa'ida worthy of respect? If everything is respectable, then the word has no meaning. To tell the truth is to point out that not every view is respectable. But that would offend some people, and the truth-teller would lose their votes.

From time immemorial, human beings have engaged in unceasing dialogue to discover a morality that would please everyone and offend no one. The effort has been both mind-consuming as well as time-consuming. And what is the result? Pro-choice people are back at square one, the most primitive and the least enlightened view of all, simply that one can do whatever he wants. This is not progress, but regress back to the least respectable of all views on morality. Choice is not a terminal value. Being pro-choice on abortion is not respectable. If it were, then everything would be respectable, including the Nazi invasion of Poland. Hitler was pro-choice. If Haley spoke the truth she would say, "I do not respect any view, even my own." But, being political, she is forbidden from saying that.

Joe Biden, on International Woman's Day, claimed that women need abortion so that they can reach their full potential. But the only way that women can come into the world is by not being aborted. If all pregnant women aborted so that they could realize their full potential, there would be no more women (or men), and the human race would expire leaving no one left to realize any potential. Now, if Biden was at all serious about potential, he would champion the lives of those members of the human family who have the greatest amount of potential—the unborn. A woman virtually uses up her potential as she lives. The longer she lives, the less potential she has. The child in the womb, however, has used up none of his potential.

Biden also fails to acknowledge that giving birth and being a mother exemplifies an important fulfillment of one's potential. Moreover, no woman can *fulfill* her potential. At best, she realizes certain potentials while excluding other potentials. If she becomes a basketball star, she must give up any ambition to become a teacher. Or if she works for Planned Parenthood, she must abandon life in a convent. Biden, to tell the truth, neither respects potential nor women.

Barack Obama affirmed same-sex marriage to a graduating class at the University of Southern California by stating that it was about time that a person can marry the one he loves. In so saying, he blithely skipped over the fact that he was endorsing incest, adultery, bigamy, and polygamy while neglecting mutual consent. But what he said sounded generous and progressive to the unthinking masses. Does Obama believe in his own rhetoric? Is he a master of self-obfuscation?

Jesus Christ is far from being a politician. That is because, for one good reason, He insisted on telling the truth. And the truths He proposes are hard truths which are easily rejected. We do not hear politicians telling people that they must die to themselves before they can become fully alive, or that they will be humbled if they dare to exalt themselves. They do not advise people to love their enemies or to pick up their cross on a daily basis. The hard sayings are not to be found in the politician's handbook of how to win friends and influence people.

The irony, however, is that the hard sayings that Christ proposes has kept Christianity going for more than 2,000 years, while the typical politician, if elected to office, seldom lasts for more than one term. The hard sayings may be rejectable, but when accepted, prove nourishing. Political platitudes are indigestible, no matter how appealing they seem at first blush.

The truth allows us to be free, particularly free from the enslavement of the lie which politicians so often deliver under the guise of making us free. Can a politician dare to tell the truth? Yes, if he wants to enlighten people. No, if he wants to be elected.

Canada and the Culture of Death

G. K. Chesterton once said that the difference between the liberals and the conservatives is that the former make mistakes which the latter are unable to correct. The master of the paradox did not have Canada in mind when he penned these words. Nonetheless, they depict the Canadian political situation more accurately than what we hear from any Canadian politician.

It took a stout-hearted American to explain to his neighbors to the north how dire their situation is. Tucker Carlson, the anchor of Tucker Carlson Tonight on the Fox network, spoke in Calgary and in Edmonton on January 24th and 25th, 2024, to read an urgent message to all Canadians. In a phrase that could be regarded as Chestertonian, he said, "I know that in Canada, it is official policy that coming out of the closet is good, unless you're the prime minister." The chorus of laughter was a reliable indication that Mr. Tucker was on the right track, though the liberals in the audience may have squirmed more than a little.

After lauding the physical beauty of the country and the politeness of the people, Carlson urged Canadians to "resist Justin Trudeau and his government to the maximum extent of your ability." "This is not a political debate," he went on to say, "This is a destruction of you and your culture and your beliefs and your children and your future." Carlson was speaking as a good neighbor, though what he had to say would not be easy to digest.

Carlson's advice did not set well with Employment Minister Randy Boissonnault who castigated Alberta's Prime Minister, Danielle Smith, for inviting him to speak. "It's deplorable," he ranted, "and we won't stand for it." Well, the audience did sit for it, and many found it to be a fair portrait of the Canadian situation.

"Your attitudes need to change and your timidity needs to be replaced by bravery," Carlson charged. At this point, his words echoed those of Alexander Solzhenitsyn who, in his 1978 Harvard address, identified himself as a friend who felt the need to point out that Americans needed to have more courage. Though his message was rejected at the time, it proved to be prophetic, and it still ranks as one of the best moral critiques of Western culture and atheistic Humanism.

Getting to the specifics, Carlson questioned why a government would make dangerous drugs available to children, noting "if someone is giving fentanyl to your children without telling you, they're trying to kill your children." He also blasted euthanasia being promoted under the euphemism of MAiD (Medical Assistance in Dying). He also condemned the erosion of civil liberties under the liberal government and its near capture of the entire media sphere by the government.

Concluding his presentation in Calgary, Carlson referred to the plight of Christians in Canada. "There's kind of no more inoffensive and peaceful group in the world than the Christians... In fact... their religion commands them to turn the other cheek and put the concerns of the country above their own." He alluded to the spate of church burnings across the country. "If you think that preaching the Gospel is so dangerous that the people who do it need to be in prison, in shackles, you're serving someone other than the people of Canada."

Climate Minister Steven Guilbeault found Carlson's remarks "hateful and violent." The Minister of Transport insisted that Carlson's speech should not have been allowed to occur. On the other side of the ledger, however, his speech was well received by the audiences of 4,000 in Calgary and nearly 10,000 in Edmonton.

The plain facts support Tucker Carlson. Last year, more than 2,000 citizens in British Columbia died of drug overdose. There were more than 13,200 cases of euthanasia in 2022, an increase of over 30% over the previous year, and the number has been steadily climbing. Over the last five years, 58,000 Canadians died while waiting for medical care. The crisis in medical care could be abated if Prime Minister Trudeau was not sending hundreds of millions of dollars to promote abortion overseas. Abortion is said to be a "right," and it is emphatically not a "right," either morally or legally. The prejudice against Catholics and pro-life people is palpable whereas members of the LGBQ consortium are treated as royalty.

Canada is presently living a Culture of Death, what Pope Saint John Paul II denounced in his 1995 encyclical *Evangelium Vitae* (The Gospel of Life) and is more and more resembling Orwell's *1984* dystopia. Mr. Carlson could have added that at the current moment in Canada, truth is hate-speech, friends are enemies, and common sense is tyranny.

Tucker Carlson's words were met with "cognitive dissonance" among the liberal politicians. They were not disposed to accept the reasonableness of what they heard. They labelled the truth they heard as a lie and the common sense that was proposed as "dangerous rhetoric." But they remain numb to their own dangerous rhetoric that they spew on a daily basis.

Christ told the truth and was put to death for it. The truth may be disagreeable, but it is the only road to freedom. Winston Churchill once said that "The Truth is incontrovertible. Malice may attack it, ignorance may deride it, but in the end, there it is."

One wonders how Canadian liberals might have reacted to an honest assessment of their country by Britain's blustery Prime Minister of long ago.

II

Prejudice vs. Justice

None Are So Blind

The account in John 9:1-39 concerning the miraculous restoration of the sight of a man born blind attests to both the power of Jesus and the obtuseness of human beings.

As He was passing by, Jesus met a man who was blind from birth. His disciples asked whether this affliction was due to his sin or that of his parents. "Neither has this man sinned nor his parents," responded Jesus, "but the works of God were to be made manifest in him . . . As long as I am in the world I am the light of the world." After saying these words, Jesus spat on the ground and made clay with the spittle and spread the clay over the man's eyes. Then he bade him to wash in the pool of Siloe. The man did as he was directed and returned in full possession of his sight.

The miracle caused some confusion among the neighbors. Was this the same man "who used to sit and beg?" some asked. The man said, "I am he." He was then taken to the Pharisees for further questioning. Some of them, however, rejected his testimony saying that "This man is not from God, for he does not keep the Sabbath." They were resorting to a technicality to dismiss an obviosity.

The miracle, in one sense, was too extraordinary to believe, but in addition to that, the Pharisees were unwilling to acknowledge that Jesus was the person He claimed to be. Their ruling status was being threatened. This was something that they could not surrender. The man whose sight was restored was then taken to his parents who were asked, "Is this your son, of whom, you say that he was born blind? How then does he now see?" The parents, however, were justifiably fearful and said, "He is of age; question him."

The man becomes subject to abuse and ultimately banished from the community. The interrogators had little interest in the facts of the case. Their strategy was to withhold official recognition of the healing by slandering Jesus in order to cover up the miracle. They made it all too clear, however, that they were unwilling to see what actually transpired. Accordingly, Jesus says, "For judgment have I come into this world, that they who do not see, may see and they who see may become blind." Restoring the sight of the man born blind was an example, though highly dramatic, of Jesus' desire to restore the spiritual sight of others.

The Pharisees, scribes, and high priests were imprisoned by their assumptions of superiority. Hence, they were incapable of seeing either their own vanity or the divinity of Jesus. The lower class, having no such assumptions, were better able to see what is essential. In this sense, Jesus can proclaim, "Blessed are the poor in spirit' (Matthew 5:3).

The intellectual blindness exhibited by the Pharisees and others in the account of the man born blind whose sight was miraculously restored, offers a prototype and a parable for a better understanding of the same blindness that afflicts various groups in the contemporary world. This group blindness inevitably makes dialogue unlikely.

Three groups in particular suffer from this specific form of blindness. In each case, there is a withdrawing from reality because of a fear. This fear prevents them from any honest discussion with their opponents.

The first is radical feminism. This ideology (and it is not a philosophy) is characterized by a rejection of the patriarchy which, if it were carried to its logical conclusion, would be self-destructive. It also includes a rejection or degradation of men along with the delusion that a woman is an independent, solo entity. Feminism has effectively barricaded itself against criticism. Despite its absence of reasonableness, however, it remains enormously influential.

The second group, the pro-abortion lobby, is also built on a false premise. It denies the human reality of the unborn, elevates choice to a self-justifying principle, and defames anyone who offers reasonable criticism. It remains wilfully blind to the devastating effects that abortion has on women, men, and the family. It flies in the face of everything we know about embryology, fetology, sociology, and psychology. It is an island unto itself and brooks no criticism.

The third group consists of atheists who, as a matter of course, reject God. This rejection leaves them with very little truth with which to defend their position. Yet, the more formidable atheists of the modern world—Marx, Stalin, Lenin, Hitler, Feuerbach, Comte, Freud, Sartre, Nietzsche, Darwin—have been unreachable and unrelenting in their fidelity to their no-God philosophy. Their hostility to religion has been an unhappy side-effect of their atheistic outlook.

Trying to communicate with representatives of any of these three groups can be frustrating and futile. Jesus experienced this problem with the Pharisees and other leaders who closed themselves off from anything challenging. We learn from Jesus about the supreme importance of humility, not to take oneself too seriously, and to avoid a group mentality that is closed to anything different from itself. We also learn something about patience, understanding, and forgiveness. We learn that none are so blind as those who refuse to see. And we look into ourselves and discover how much darkness is there. We invite the light of Jesus as we try to remove the darkness in ourselves.

Love Is Sweeping the Country

The day after Christmas in 1931, George Gershwin (with lyrics by his brother, Ira) released "Love is Sweeping the Country." Both the music and lyrics swelled with optimism: "Love is sweeping the country/waves are hugging the shore/all the sexes from Maine to Texas/have never known such love before." Ira Gershwin could be forgiven for implying a multitude of sexes. It was all part of the dizzy excitement caused by an alleged flood tide of love.

Well, that's popular music. Tunes may be catchy, but they are not always convincing. In today's world, I would venture to think that it is not love but self-righteousness that is sweeping the country. Charles Spurgeon, known for his sermons, poetry, and hymns, once said that "the greatest enemy to human souls is the self-righteous spirit which makes men look to themselves for salvation." That single sentence is a salutary sermon in itself.

As destructive as self-righteousness can be, it is just as difficult to diagnose in the self. A person may be able to see the speck in the other's eye but remain oblivious to the log in his own. Self-righteousness is virtually a synonym for the deadly sin of pride. In fact, it feeds off pride. Its logical antidote, therefore, is humility. And it seems clear enough that humility is not sweeping the country.

Everyone wants to make the world a better place. A phrase in a typical eulogy is, "He made the world a better place." Trying to make the world a better place, however, runs up against a multitude of others who are busy trying to make the world a more troublesome place than it already is. Competing against the drift of the world is beyond the meager capacities of the individual who, like Don Quixote, remains a dreamer. Nonetheless, each person is called to perform whatever good lies within his capacities. We are asked, as Mother Teresa is known to have said, to be faithful.

The self-righteous person is constantly on the lookout for breaches of conduct. And he finds them everywhere. Mathematics, for some of the eagle-eyed detectives, is racist. And so are all whites. Someone who stands by a view that is counter to the thought police is routinely branded as racist, sexist, homophobic, anti-trans, or being guilty of 'hate speech' for telling the truth (being labeled 'conservative' might be the most defamatory of all accusations). College students are taught to be sensitive to 'micro-aggressions' such as 'where do you come from'? or 'how old are you?' or stating that there are but two sexes. One professor preaches that the proper way to respond to a micro-aggression is by a 'macro-aggression.' These approaches are not exactly paving the way to a better world. A strong denunciation is the politically correct response to an imagined slight. The apogee of political correctness and Woke is violence.

The self-righteous person wants the world to be a better place, but on his terms. And here is the problem. Putting the idea of changing the world aside for the moment, it is not likely that one self-righteous person is in a position to change another person who is equally self-righteous. Changing the world is beyond the range of anyone who is limited by self-righteousness. The center of self-righteousness is in the self, a locus not broad enough to be of any help to anyone else.

Righteousness, on the other hand, has its center in God. The Ten Commandments, issued by God, are for everyone. A good sermon should be God-centered, not ego-centered. No doubt the decline in the

Christian religion, which is based on the love of God and neighbor, has contributed to a self-centered replacement religion. Christianity, like its founder, who is "meek and humble of heart" preaches and teaches humility. Pride is currently celebrated with shameless audacity.

Charles Livingstone Allen (1913-2005), a United Methodist preacher who presided over the largest congregation in the state of Georgia, has a stinging message for the self-righteous: "The hardest people to reach with the love of God are not the bad people. They know they are bad. They have no defense. The hardest ones to win for God are the self-righteous people."

Another factor in the rise of self-righteousness is the decline of philosophy. The love of wisdom has largely been co-opted by a variety of pseudo-philosophies that have no objective center, such as deconstruction, relativism, skepticism, and nihilism. As the poet William Butler Yeats describes the situation, "the centre cannot hold; mere anarchy is loosed upon the world . . . The best lack all conviction, while the worst are full of passionate intensity."

Philosophical lassitude has swept the country while those appointed to leadership positions are not leading. Only God can help, but He is not being called upon. There are now passages in the Bible that are presently deemed criminal. In which direction can people turn without being vilified?

C. S. Lewis has wisely and deftly pointed out that "humility is not thinking less of yourself; but thinking of yourself less." With humility one has nothing to lose and everything to gain. It keeps self-righteousness at bay while taking full advantage of the positive self who understands both his attributes as well as his limitations. Humility anchors love since it recognizes the debt it owes to others. It is, therefore, congenial with altruism, which is another name for love.

If love ever does "sweep the country," it is only because humility has defeated self-centeredness and, along with it, self-righteousness.

Making People Feel Good about Being Bad

Making people feel good about being bad is the corollary of making people feel bad about being good. In C. S. Lewis' *The Screwtape Letters*, the devil takes pride is getting people to classify being good as a form of "Puritanism." "And may I remark in passing," he writes, "that the value we have given to that word is one of the really solid triumphs of the last hundred years?" "Goodie-two-shoes," "prudes," "Victorian," and "holier than thou" have been equally effective in making people experience shame about being good.

It is a common experience for young boys to be made to feel "out of it" or even timid if they do not smoke, swear, or steal. The temptation to be good is made all the more difficult by the pressure to conform to the ring leaders.

The attempt to make decent people feel bad about their own decency is also an attempt for indecent people to feel good about their own indecency. The "pride" parade is a perfect example of people purporting to be proud of their sexual transgressions while condemning their critics as being "homophobic." Abortion has been identified as an act of love while pro-life people are routinely condemned for presumably lacking compassion.

To maintain one's moral standards in the face of ridicule requires courage. It also requires tolerance and even forgiveness toward one's detractors. In the final analysis, the virtuous person can become indebted to his critics for making him even more virtuous.

Pope Francis has caused a stir by approving, in *Fiducia Supplicans*, blessings for same-sex couples. One of his most enthusiastic disciples in this matter is Fr. James Martin, S. J., who is most pleased to bless couples who "love one another." Soon after the publication of *Fiducia Supplicans*, on December 18, 2023, Fr. Martin administered the first public blessing of a same-sex couple at his Jesuit residence in New York City.

The Bible, as well as the Catholic Catechism, make it clear that homosexual acts are sinful. It would seem obvious that two people who are encouraging each other to sin are, by their actions, expressing something other than love. Love promotes the good of the other. Love is not the promotion of sin. Fr. Martin seems to be saying, "go and sin some more." Moreover, sin on a continuing basis. By contrast, Christ said to the woman who was caught in adultery, "Go thy way, and from now on sin no more" (John 8:11).

The purpose of a blessing is to provide the grace needed to avoid sin. This cannot be the case with regard to blessing same-sex couples. What then, is the purpose of such blessings? It is, it would seem, simply to make the couple feel good about what they are doing. It is to make people feel good about being bad. This, we might say, is more devilish than godly.

It makes no sense to bless a person who is intent on robbing a bank. The thief might welcome the blessing because it makes him feel better about his lifestyle. But the blessing is not aimed at preventing him from his nefarious act. It is, simply, to make him feel good. It would appear even more ludicrous if the blessing were conferred by the president of a bank.

Jane Fonda once remarked that adultery cannot be so bad if it makes me feel so good. Moral acts, however, are not about feelings. They are about the nature of the moral act. One might feel triumphant after getting away with robbing a bank. Many motion pictures have presented the thief as a hero. Thoughtful people may question the moral actions of Robin Hood. Feelings can be fickle. They provide a most unreliable basis for morality. They replace what is objective with something that is subjective. In the story of *Ali Baba and the Forty Thieves*, the robbers are confirmed in their way of life. They approve robbery for themselves but seek revenge against Ali Baba for taking some of their treasure. They insist that others be moral, but not themselves. Members of the Mafia do not disdain treachery, arson, and murder.

Making a person feel good about being bad actually serves as a preventative for being good. Being comfortable in one's sin takes away an incentive for being good. Being comfortable about one's sins is moral inertia. The purpose of a blessing is to abandon sin and choose what is good.

A person who does not commit grievous sins might feel comfortable in the fact that his sins are but venial. This is a dangerous deception. Venial sins can be a prelude to those of a more grievous kind. Nonetheless, a life of relatively small sins can be sufficient to cost a person his soul. As Screwtape advises his apprentice nephew, "Indeed, the safest road to Hell is the gradual one—the gentle slope, soft underfoot, without sudden turnings, without milestones, without signposts." "Be thou perfect, as thy heavenly Father is perfect" is sound advice.

Feeling good can dull a person's conscience. We do not help others by offering sedatives, but incentives. If Christ comes with a sword (Matthew 10:34-36), it is to arouse us from our complacency since we have more important things to accomplish. The life that is unchallenged will lead to regret. We all need to be told when we are wrong that we are wrong. Sugar coating is as dangerous as a narcotic.

Religious Bigotry and the Constitution

The United States Constitution is quite friendly toward Catholics as well as toward all people who hold religious beliefs. Article VI, clause 3, states that "no religious Test shall ever be required as a Qualification to any Office or public Trust under the United States."

In a 1787 article defending the necessity of the Constitution's ban on religious tests, Oliver Ellsworth, third Chief Justice of the Supreme Court, defined a religious test as an act to be done, among other things, "for the purpose of determining whether his religious opinions are such that he is admissible to a public office." This clause is cited by advocates of separation of church and state as an example of the "original intent" of the framers of the constitution to avoid any confusion concerning the boundaries of the church and the state, or involving the government in any way as a determiner of religious beliefs or practices. The secular world cannot ordain Catholic priests, nor can the church appoint secular officials. This clause is also significant because it represents the words of the original Framers, even prior to the Establishment Clause of the First Amendment.

By dramatic contrast, a variety of Test Acts were instituted in England during the 17th and 18th centuries. Their main purpose was to exclude anyone not a member of the Church of England from holding government office (notably Catholics and "non-conforming Protestants). Government officials were required to swear oaths, such as the Oath of Supremacy, attesting that the monarch of England was the head of the Church and that they possessed no other foreign loyalties, such as to the pope. Such laws were common throughout Europe, wherever countries had a state religion.

The United States Constitution forbids such a Test. Therefore, a person cannot be disqualified from assuming an official post because he is Catholic or a member of any other religion. Nonetheless, Act VI, clause 3 is not always honored in practice. During the 2020 senate hearing concerning Amy Coney Barrett's confirmation to the Supreme Court, her Catholicism was questioned. California Senator Dianne Feinstein stated that the candidate's Catholicism was a problem. "The dogma lives loudly within you," she said, "and that's of concern." Coney Barrett was confirmed by a vote of 52-48. All the Republicans except one voted in her favor, while all the Democrats and the two Independents voted against her.

Had Feinstein violated the Constitution's Article VI, clause three? Some critics believed her questioning was both unconstitutional as well as anti-Catholic. Feinstein defended herself by insisting that Barrett's writings were informed by her faith and thus were an obstacle to her service to her country. The great merit of the Constitution's ban on using a religious Test to determine a candidate's suitability for office is that it is a barrier against prejudice. A person's faith in God, for example, does not mean that he is incapable of serving the cause of justice. At the same time, a person's color does not indicate his proficiency or insufficiency in other areas. "Let us judge people not by the color of their skin, but by the content of their character," said Martin Luther King.

As Vice-President, Mike Pence once put senator Kamala Harris on the spot for her attacks on the religious views of several recent judicial nominees. "Senator," he said, "I know one of our judicial nominees you actually attacked, because they [sic] were a member of the Catholic Knights of Columbus just because the Knights of Columbus hold pro-life views. My hope is that when the hearing [Supreme Court Justice nomination] takes place that Judge Amy Coney Barrett will be respectfully voted and confirmed onto the Supreme Court of the United States." Harris voted against Barrett's confirmation. Questioning the suitability for office because of one's religious beliefs, however, is not uncommon in the world of politics.

In late 2018, Kamala Harris grilled Brian Buescher, who was nominated to be a federal district judge in Nebraska, about his membership in the Knights of Columbus, a Catholic fraternal organization with more than 2 million members worldwide that conducts charitable work. The following is one of Harris's written questions to Buescher:

> "Since 1993, you have been a member of the Knights of Columbus, an all-male society comprised primarily of Catholic men. In 2016, Carl Anderson, leader of the Knights of Columbus, described abortion as 'a legal regime that has resulted in more than 40 million deaths.' Mr. Anderson went on to say that 'abortion is the killing of the innocent on a massive scale.' Were you

aware that the Knights of Columbus opposed a woman's right to choose when you joined the organization?"

Harris is trying to make Buescher out to be sexist as well as misogynist. Harris sees no room for opinions other than her own. She is either ignorant or defiant of the Constitution that protects people from this kind of prejudice. Not only is a pro-life person suitable for a judiciary position, but in defending the rights of the unborn, he is particularly suitable. The United States Constitution, the supreme law of America, protects people from the likes of Dianne Feinstein, Kamala Harris, and others. Unfortunately, religious bigotry, especially against Catholics, persists among high-ranking politicians whose attitudes are more pharisaical than fair-minded, more prejudicial than prudential.

Is Christianity for the Birds?

The crisis in the Church today is of considerable magnitude. We have nominal Catholics zealously promoting abortion, a Cardinal who wants to have the Marian apparitions cancelled, bishops approving blessings for same-sex marriages, a pope who writes the preface to a book written by a priest whose main apostolate is to justify homosexual acts, while hundreds of Catholic churches have been vandalized. On the surface of things, it appears that Christianity has become a battlefield for her enemies who seem to be winning the fight. But will the enemy inherit the Church?

In the parable of the mustard seed (Matthew 13:31-32), Christ states that "the kingdom of heaven is like a mustard seed, which a man took and planted in his field. Though it is the smallest of all seeds, yet when it grows, it is the largest of garden plants and becomes a tree, so that the birds come and perch in its branches."

The parable is also a prophecy. Christianity was very small in its infancy but grew and spread throughout the world in large numbers. History confirms this. A comparison can be made with the human organism which begins as a one-cell zygote and grows prolifically until it reaches around 37 billion cells in the adult. Wondrous things can emerge from small beginnings. Humility is the virtue that recognizes our smallness, but not our insignificance. The humble person, like the mustard seed, is the basis for a moral growth that produces a human who is the glory of God. Simply stated, great things can come from small beginnings.

The tree that grows from a mustard seed invites birds to occupy its branches. There are different translations concerning the way in which birds "perch" in the tree. Alternate descriptions employ the words "dwell" and "nest." These terms suggest that the birds and their progeny will remain in the tree for the duration.

In a comparable parable (Mark 4:3-9), Christ states, "Listen! Behold, a sower went out to sow. And as he sowed, some seed fell along the path, and the birds came and devoured it. Other seed fell on rocky ground, where it did not have much soil, and immediately it sprang up, since it had no depth of soil. And when the sun rose, it was scorched, and since it had no root, it withered away. Other seed fell among thorns, and the thorns grew up and choked it, and it yielded no grain. And other seeds fell into good soil and produced grain, growing up and increasing and yielding thirtyfold and sixtyfold and a hundredfold." And he said, "He who has ears to hear, let him hear."

The reference to the birds in both parables is of importance. If we relate both parables to each other, we conclude that in both instances, the birds symbolize a problem for the Church. In the first case, they inhabit the Church despite the fact that the Church is growing. In the second instance, the birds are seen as preventing the Church from growing. Therefore, Christianity has enemies, symbolized by the birds, not only at its foundation, but also as it is growing. It has enemies at both fronts, to use a military term. Christianity cannot rest.

Christianity survived the assaults against it in ancient Rome. The crisis in today's world takes place after Christianity has existed for more than 2,000 years. There is hardly any reason to be complacent. Christians must be eternally vigilant.

Concerning the parable according to Mark, the Word of God could not develop unless it had some depth. Attempts in the modern world are all too frequent to replace philosophies and theologies that have depth with the superficial ideologies of the day. Such ideologies, because of their lack of depth, will not last. However, in the meantime they can do a great deal of damage. The Church of "nice" is not the Church of Christ.

Secondly, the "thorns" represent ideas that are antagonistic to faith, hope, and charity, viable ideas that are the building blocks of Christianity. The secular world, by placing its faith in today, has no hope for a future with God. The cult of selfishness is a direct enemy of a love of neighbor that transcends selfishness. Those committed to the secular world will not see or hear the goodness of good ideas. Hence, Christ advises that, "He who has ears let him hear."

In these two parables, Christ has warned us against our enemies. Christianity is not for the birds, but for those who plant a seed that will grow and be safeguarded in its development. At the same time, the parables convey a great deal of hope. Great things will emerge, despite the enemies that abound, when we plant the right seed in the right soil. We should not be discouraged or overwhelmed by our enemies.

Christ has provided us with a formula for success. We should not make accommodations to our enemies but remain firm in our faith. The New Testament, not the daily newspaper, should be our guide. We should live by the Word of God and not by the weeds of today.

In the parable of the weeds, Christ states that "the field is the world; the good seed, the sons of the kingdom; the weeds, the sons of the wicked one; and the enemy who sowed them is the devil. But the harvest is the end of the world, and the reapers are the angels" (Matthew 13; 38-39).

III

Vice vs. Virtue

Is Tolerance a Virtue?

Tolerance lies somewhere between condemnation and approval. It operates within a spacious territory that ranges from tolerating another person's peculiar way of sneezing to tolerating an injustice. In most cases tolerance is not an issue. It is something we need on an every-day basis. But it becomes an issue when a person does nothing in the face of evil.

For St. Thomas Aquinas, love is the form of all virtues. Therefore, when a virtue is expressed, it directs love to another person. In this regard, virtue is an action. Tolerance, on the other hand, refrains from action and on this basis does not qualify as a virtue. Tolerance, indeed, backs away from acting.

Tolerance is an acceptable stance when there is nothing a person can do about a bad situation or when tolerance can make the situation worse. Accordingly, Aquinas states that "those who are in authority, rightly tolerate certain evils, lest certain goods be lost, or certain greater evils be incurred."

In 1920, the United States prohibited the production, importation, transportation, and sale of alcohol.

The Prohibition Era ended in 1933 because ignoring the law became more and more socially acceptable, organized crime along with violence was on the increase, and public opposition to Prohibition became overwhelming. This was a dramatic case where the failure to tolerate a situation (the recreational use of alcohol), perhaps even a vice, produced one that was significantly worse.

Amplifying his position, Aquinas states the following: "Now human law is framed for a number of human beings, the majority of whom are not perfect in virtue. Wherefore, human laws do not forbid all vices, from which the virtuous abstain, but only the more grievous vices, from which it is possible for the majority to abstain; and chiefly those that are to the hurt of others, without the prohibition of which human society could not be maintained: thus human law prohibits murder, theft, and such like (*Summa Theologica*, I-II, Q. 96, a. 1)."

There is much room for tolerance with regard to the petty vices of the many who have not as yet achieved a virtuous life. One must have prudence (which is a virtue) to know when to act and when to be tolerant.

Even God is tolerant in certain instances. For the Angelic Doctor, "although God is all-powerful and supremely good, nevertheless He allows certain evils to take place in the universe, which He might prevent, lest, without them, greater goods might be forfeited, or greater evils ensue." God would become unbearable if He punished every peccadillo.

The question now turns to how one should respond to grave evils. Abortion must be considered as a grave evil because it is the willful destruction of an innocent human being. And here is a problem of profound contemporary significance. Should we simply tolerate abortion, or should we do something about it?

The attitude of many, including Catholics, is that with regard to abortion we should respect the choice that a woman has made and mind our own business. We should not try to impose our will on another. Tolerance, in this sense, is elevated to the status of a virtue. But in the face of a grave evil, this form of tolerance is morally unacceptable. To tolerate abortion is to fail to recognize the obligations we all have toward our neighbor. It should be clear to Christians, in particular, that they cannot tolerate a neighbor's involvement in a soul-destructive activity. Even the Roman poet, Terence, a pagan, understood this. His trenchant words have survived the centuries: "I am a human being; I consider nothing human alien to me" (*Homo sum, humani nihil a me alienum puto*). A more contemporary poet, G. K. Chesterton, put it this way: "*We* men and women are all in the same boat, upon a stormy sea. *We owe* to *each other* a terrible and tragic *loyalty*."

What can one do other than tolerate abortion? One can always pray. But there are many things a conscientious person can do to protest abortion, morally, actively, financially, intellectually, and by his association with any number of groups that, collectively, are doing their best to send the message to the public of the sanctity of life and the brotherhood of man.

To do nothing in the face of evil is not a virtue, but it is the absence of one, namely, courage. The fear of "imposing one's private views" is not a justification for cowardice. Nor is the reluctance to "judge" an excuse for inaction. We owe a "terrible and tragic" duty to others because that duty demands a host of virtues that are not easily obtained: justice, courage, prudence, hope, and loyalty.

To be tolerant of a grave evil is to sit on the sidelines and refuse to enter the game. The game, of course, presents heavy demands that include rejection and ridicule. One will either win or lose, but he cannot win unless he plays the game. The game of which we are speaking here is the "game" of life. To cite Chesterton once again, "Tolerance is the virtue of the man without convictions."

There are many things in life that are intolerable. But no human being is unlovable. And that is why tolerance is not a virtue. It is supremely unhelpful. At the same time, legitimate tolerance must be guided by prudence so that it avoids the twin vices of moral inertia and fanaticism.

Is Trusting Others a Form of Love?

Some people who favor abortion believe that this complex issue can be resolved simply by trusting women. This strategy has considerable appeal since it places confidence in all women and is furthest removed from any hint of misogyny. On the other hand, many women come to regret having had an abortion, realizing that the women who advised them were not trustworthy.

We are living in the age of scam. Millions of unsuspecting people are bilked of considerable sums of money because they trusted deceiving scam artists. Not a day passes without the telephone, the mail, or the computer being used by thieves to rob people. The overwhelming evidence tells us that we should be careful whom we trust. "In God we trust," which is inscribed on coins, is an aphorism suggesting that God can be trusted and no one else. A pundit reinforced this advice by adding, "Everyone else pays cash." Sadly, as novelist Stephen King as said, "The trust of the innocent is the liar's most useful tool."

Abraham Lincoln, who was a fountain of good advice, once said, "Fool me once, shame on you; fool me twice, shame on me." Just as a person is innocent until proven guilty, a person may be trustworthy until he proves otherwise. We should be on guard against people trying to deceive us. A more recent president, Ronald Reagan, said, in the tradition of Lincoln, "Trust, but verify."

Christ commanded us to love our neighbor, but He did not command us to trust him. Each person, created by God, is lovable. But not everyone is trustworthy. Trustworthiness is something that a person must earn. We are lovable since we were created by a loving God.

Euripides' play, *Hecuba*, is the tragedy of a person who trusted a friend who turned out to be ruthlessly untrustworthy. In the Greek legend, Hecuba was the principal wife of the Trojan king, Priam. As a result of the Greeks capturing Troy, Hecuba was dethroned, dispossessed of her fortune, and imprisoned. In order to secure the safety of her youngest son, Polydorus, she entrusted him to the care of Polymestor, the king of Thrace. Her trust, however, was tragically misplaced. She discovered that her son was murdered. Hecuba had borne many deprivations without losing her moral integrity. But she could not bear the murder of her son. She snapped. "I am now no longer human; I am a dog." In revenge, she put out the eyes of Polymestor and murdered his two sons. The realization that she had entrusted her son to a murderer was too much for her to bear.

Betraying a trust is contrary to love. It can be a grievous offense against friendship and brings to mind the betrayal of Judas. Yet, betrayal should not lead to revenge, but to forgiveness. The notion of trust brings into focus a host of moral categories and has been a recurring theme throughout literature.

We are obliged to find out whether the people we trust are truly trustworthy. Here is where the virtue of prudence comes into play. Avoiding this obligation is a fault, specifically, the deadly sin of sloth. Trusting everyone is a case of extreme naiveté. On the other hand, deciding never to trust anyone is the despair of cynicism.

Friendship is the happy occasion when trust between two persons is reciprocal. It cannot abide betrayal or any sign of inconsistency. Therefore, it must be rare. "Love all, trust few, do wrong to none," wrote Shakespeare.

The question arises, "Can I trust myself?" Being able to trust one's self is the shining virtue of integrity. It is an important question. Can a person trust himself after a few drinks, or putting himself in a seductive environment? We should be aware of our limitations and not be led into temptation. We are never without the need for grace.

Many summers ago, I tried my luck as a door-to-door encyclopedia salesman. I considered myself a trustworthy vendor of a trustworthy product. I encountered a lady who wanted what I had to sell but had been "burned" a few times and could no longer trust any salesman. Try as I may, I could not convince her that I was entirely trustworthy. The misleading merchants who preceded me had collectively defeated any argument I had to clear myself of suspicion. It is an unhappy thought to be perceived by others as untrustworthy.

We find in our own day, the Church being seen as untrustworthy, while other agencies, that are entirely untrustworthy, are eagerly invited into people's homes and hearts. Prejudice is often the barrier that prevents people from seeing the trustworthiness of what is trustworthy. In such cases, all we can do is to recommit ourselves to being trustworthy and hope that it will radiate. In *The Merchant of Venice*, Shakespeare states, "How far that candle throws its beams! So shines a good deed in a naughty world."

Endeavor to be trustworthy and you will ultimately make friends. Others will need to stand in line. The one person we have the best chance of changing is our selves. And yet, we can find a hundred rationalizations for deferring the job. Ralph Waldo Emerson, at one time America's most quotable author, held "self-reliance" as the most important virtue. There is no such thing, however, as a "self-made man." We need honest introspection, but we also need to have trust in God, which is to say, a reliance on the One who cannot be untrustworthy.

Is Naiveté a Vice or a Virtue?

Naiveté has the semblance of virtue since it is based on trusting others. Trusting others seems to be a form of good will. However, Christ did not command us to trust others, but to love them, even those who are our enemies. This is because each person, created by God, is lovable, though not every person is trustworthy.

Nor is naiveté a vice. In most instances, it is innocent and harmless. It is certainly not confessable. Nonetheless, it may acquiesce to vice. It renders a person highly susceptible, on certain occasions, to being exploited. The word "scam," familiar to anyone who has a computer, attests to the fact that millions of people each year fall prey scam schemers on the mistaken belief that they are dealing with people who are trustworthy.

Because naiveté can lead people into trouble, it is prudent for them to understand the dangers of being overly naïve. While naiveté itself is not a virtue, it cries out for the virtue of prudence. On the other hand, in trusting no one, a person lapses into cynicism, which is a vice. Ignoring naiveté, when it becomes clear that it causes harm, is wilful blindness or sloth which is also a vice. Whereas naiveté is not a vice, it is surrounded by both vices and virtues.

President Franklin Delano Roosevelt was being inexcusably naïve when he said that Stalin ("Uncle Joe") was trustworthy. At the same time, among the "Big Three," Churchill was being prudent by not trusting Stalin at all, whereas Stalin was being cynical by not trusting anyone.

When Malcolm Muggeridge was Rector at Edinburgh University, he was rebuked by the Roman Catholic chaplain for suggesting that the free distribution of contraceptives to students was conducive to promoting sexual promiscuity, he was not being naïve. But the chaplain was being most naïve in believing otherwise. In a stinging letter to Muggeridge, he penned the following words: "The plain fact is that we do not find elderly journalists with a gift of invective useful allies in presenting Christian standards." The chaplain would do well if he traded his naiveté for a little Christian charity.

There is a most dangerous form of naiveté that is currently sweeping the country. It is presenting the LGBTQ+ as a fine organization that should be accepted, promoted, and celebrated everywhere, and that its rainbow flag should be more venerated than the stars and stripes. This is a collective naiveté that has won the allegiance of the better part of the nation. And it will not abide opposition.

Our parish priest made a video in which he extolled the positive contribution that the group was making. He waxed enthusiastically about how God's love extends to people whose lifestyles are questioned. Christianity has never denied that God loves everyone. But there are the Ten Commandments that prohibit certain sexually practices. Our priest did not explain why arsonists, embezzlers, and thieves were not included in God's sweeping love. He saw only what he wanted to see, and what he saw had no connection with reality.

The LGBTQ+ consortium is intensely anti-Christian. Its activists are outraged when anyone refuses to pay them a form of homage that is demanded by no other group. Let us examine a single incident that makes the case.

Emo is a small town in Ontario that has gained notoriety because it has refused to bend to the demands of LGBTQ+ activists. It showed the temerity to reject a motion to proclaim June as "Pride" month and fly the LGBT "Pride" flag. The town council had voted 3-2 against proclaiming June as "Pride" month and flying LGBT flags from municipal buildings. As a result, the town must appear in front of a Human Rights Tribunal. The plaintiff is seeking monetary compensation in the order of $15,000 from the municipality, and $10,000 each from the mayor and two councillors who voted against the proclamation. Society has bought into a militant group with a lofty regard for its importance together with activities that border on terrorism.

Many have bought into the lie that LGBTQ+ is a "community." Such a widespread belief, however, is more akin to a kind of mass hypnosis. How can it be a "community"? In his book *The Day Is Now Spent*, Robert Cardinal Sarah states that it is politically correct now to speak of members of LGBTQ+ "as though they were a separate class of people with a common culture, a particular way of dressing and speaking, neighborhoods set aside in the cities, and even their own stores and restaurants. They are described as if they were an ethnic community."

Communities are made up of individual persons who work together for a common good. A real community does not consist of widely separated individuals who are defined by their sexual behavior. People who are left-handed do not belong to a left-handed community. Nor do heterosexuals belong to a heterosexual community. If a person is a Celtic fan, he does not belong to a Celtic community. The belief that the aforementioned group belongs to a community is a fairy tale, but one that, unfortunately, is taken to be true.

We are all, in certain ways, naïve. We are responsible, however, to know something about the consequences of our naiveté, for they may be significant. We must be prudent, avoid cynicism, and refrain from sloth. Put simply, we must beware and be wise.

Is It a Virtue to Have an Open Mind?

A writer does not need to look very far to find grist for the mill. If he has an open mind, he will find abundant opportunities to ply his trade. But if his mind remains open and never closes on anything worth communicating, he betrays his vocation. If one is open for business, he does want to close a sale or two.

I was in a drug store waiting for a prescription to be filled. This gave me time to roam the aisles to see if anything else tempted my pocketbook. I came upon an elaborate Halloween display. A row of ghoulish-looking talking heads caught my attention. I activated the voice box of one of them and listened to its eerie warning: "Don't let your mind be so open that your brains fall out." This grim enunciation was punctuated by several seconds of sardonic laughter.

Here was wisdom from a dummy that had something important to say to my students who, in general, were proud of being open-minded. But their affection for keeping their minds open was accompanied by their fear of ever closing it. I have always taught that the first lesson in philosophy is that the human brain should be activated.

The Halloween message is a paraphrase of something that Arthur Hays Sulzberger, publisher of *The New York Times* from 1935-61, once said: "I believe in an open mind, but not so open that your brains fall out." Sulzberger would be amused to learn that his esteemed vehicle of communication has now shifted from the print medium to talking Halloween heads. His point is perennial. The purpose of looking is finding. The fulfillment of being open is to discover something worth having.

Allan Bloom wrote his best-seller *The Closing of the American Mind* to explain how having a perpetually open-mind is equivalent to having no mind at all. There is no education without truth, which is something that the persistently open mind never attains. Being told in the classroom that the mind works only half-way is to immobilize the brain or, simply, to "close" it. Someone once said the "a diplomat is a man who says you have an open mind instead of telling you that you have a hole in your head." The classroom, however, should not be an

Is it a Virtue to Have an Open Mind?

arena for diplomacy. Truth may make a person uncomfortable, but there can be no education without it.

"Keep an open mind" has become a mantra for those of a liberal persuasion. It is an attitude, however, that yields no fruit. Truth, accordingly, becomes undiscoverable, and the very point of being open is meaningless. It is one thing to be independent, but one should not be independent of what he needs. Phyllis McGinley was not impressed by the person who boasted of an open mind:

> "So open was his mind, so wide
> To welcome winds from every side
> That public weather took dominion,
> Sweeping him bare of all opinion."

The human mind has not completed its natural function while remaining in the state of openness. It is only when it closes itself on something true or good or right that it has completed the activity for which it was created.

A door should open to let one in and close to keep others out. The mouth must open and close in order for eating to take place. The hand opens to grasp, closes to capture. Eyelids open so that one can see, close so that one can sleep. Life is dyadic, a system of opening and closing. So, too, the mind should close on what is worth keeping. Sir Thomas Beecham once defined great music as, "That which penetrates the ear with facility and leaves the memory with difficulty." "Magical music," he added, "never leaves the memory." We are open to good music, and when we come upon it, we want to keep it. Good music finds its home in the listener. We want to close on what we find to be beautiful. And if the word "close" is problematic, it can be replaced by welcome, accept, enjoy, or treasure. Good music ultimately belongs in the mind and heart of the listener, just as truth belongs in the mind.

There is an unfounded fear of knowing the truth of anything. The fear is to appear proud or presumptuous. This fear is unwarranted because a person who claims to know any truth must, in humility, recognize that the acquisition of truth does not make him superior but gives him the responsibility to profess it. The Catholic Church is both the teacher and guardian of truth. But it is equally zealous in promoting the virtues of humility and gratitude. No one likes a show-off. But to deny that truth can be known is to lapse into cowardice. Truth can be known; humility and gratitude can be realized.

Ray Bradbury wrote his 1953 novella *Fahrenheit 451* to show how foolish it is to avoid knowing anything for fear of appearing superior or inferior. In the story, Fireman Guy Montag holds up a copy of Aristotle's *Ethics* and explains that anyone who reads this book must feel superior for having read it. Therefore, he explains, all books must be burned so that equality among people can be preserved. An egalitarian world, however, is a dystopian world.

Having an open mind is half a virtue. And the half virtues can do more damage than a vice that has no claim to virtue. The other half of the virtue is closing the mind on what is honestly perceived to be true. One can make mistakes, but the pursuit of truth is an adventure that none of us should ever shun.

Is Marriage a Joke?

We know, of course, that marriage, the most intimate, beautiful, and enduring relationship between a man and a woman, is anything but a joke. Nonetheless, when some people look at how celebrities have misused this lofty ideal, we can understand why they might be tempted to think that it is a joke.

In the case of Tommy Manville, heir to the Johns-Manville asbestos fortune, marriage for him was surely a joke. On the occasion of his thirteenth marriage, he earned his way into the Guinness Book of Records for the greatest number of marital unions. He is mentioned in a song by Irving Berlin—*What Chance Have I with Love?*—that includes the words, "with asbestos he still gets burned." He stated, concerning one particular divorce that carried a huge cash settlement, "She cried, and the judge wiped her tears with my checkbook."

Zsa Zsa Gabor and Jennifer O'Neill tied the knot 9 times, while Lana Turner, Artie Shaw, Mickey Rooney, Elizabeth Taylor, and Larry King ventured into marriage on 8 occasions. Martha Raye and Jerry

Lee Lewis sought marital bliss for their 7th merry-go-round whereas a host of celebrities exchanged vows 6 times, including Hedy Lamarr, Boris Karloff, Stan Laurel, Claude Rains, Tony Curtis, and Rex Harrison.

G. K. Chesterton was amused by those critics of marriage who found it to be unrealistic. "They appear to imagine," he wrote, "that the ideal of constancy was a joke mysteriously imposed on mankind by the devil, instead of being, as it is, a yoke consistently imposed on all lovers by themselves."

Aristotle remarked that "the corruption of the best is the worst." When marriage fails, it falls from a great height. It should not be judged by its failure, however, but by its fullness. There are enough failures, however, for marriage to serve as the butt of humor: "Marriage is not a word, but a sentence;" "Wedlock is padlock"; "Marriage ties the knot, divorce unties it." "Socrates died of an overdose of wedlock;" "The plural of spouse is spice." Benjamin Disraeli added to the fun by recommending that every woman should marry and no man.

Pope Saint John Paul II began his "theology of the body" with a text from St. Matthew (19:3ff.). A group of Pharisees approached Christ and asked him whether it is lawful for a man to divorce his wife for any reason. Christ's answer must have been very disappointing to his questioners: "Have you not read that he who made them from the beginning made them male and female and said, 'For this reason a man should leave his father and mother and be joined to his wife, and the two shall become one flesh. What therefore God has joined together, let not man put asunder'."

Not being satisfied with Christ's response, the Pharisees asked why Moses allowed divorce. Then Christ said to them, "For your hardness of heart, Moses allowed you to divorce your wives, but from the beginning it was not so."

The "beginning" is described in the first book of the Bible. Genesis 2:24 establishes the principle of unity between man and woman as the very content of the Word of God as it is expressed in the most ancient revelation. One cannot argue with God. Marriage is an intimate union between a man and a woman and is indissoluble. This is decisive!

Christ answers the Pharisees. But at the same time, he is speaking to everyone so that what is demanded of marriage is clear to all. As John Paul remarks, "we must put ourselves precisely in the position of Christ's interlocutors today. Marriage has not changed, though many have sought a less demanding substitute."

The nature of marriage, as stated in Genesis, rules out contraception and abortion. Contraception would deny the bodily unity of the husband and wife. It would also deny the fruitfulness of the marital union which is the conception of the child. In addition, the fruit of the marital union cannot be death, but life. Therefore, the adoption of contraception and abortion contradicts the essence of marriage.

Also, as Christ told the Pharisees, marriage is indissoluble. Divorce violates the indissolubility of marriage. So, too, adultery violates the two-in-one flesh unity of marriage. Moreover, the heart must have a definitive role. As Christ remarked, Moses allowed divorce because of a certain "hardness of the heart." Marriage, therefore, is about love, specifically the kind of total commitment that continues until death.

The essence of a joke is to bring something down from its lofty perch, such as in the aforementioned examples about marriage. All the jokes about sex involve reducing it to something far less than it is, often to something bawdy. The redeeming value of a joke, on the other hand, is that it is not to be taken seriously. But there is no redeeming value to making a joke out of marriage by reducing it to a charade, a sham, a travesty of what it should be. Those who enter marriage without honoring its true nature will inevitably pay the price. If the price is not divorce, it may be discord, disappointment, or unhappiness.

Finally, it must be said that reading and accepting the wisdom of Genesis requires humility. Today, it seems that more people are reading the Bible with a certain critical pride that inclines them to disregard some passages and delete others. We turn once again to G. K. Chesterton who saw clearly that "pride, which is the falsification of fact by the introduction of self, is the enduring blunder of mankind."

No one should want to create a bungle out of his marriage. Only by accepting marriage in its wholeness, the way God instituted it, can we prevent that tragic descent into its disfigurement as a joke.

Part Two

Common Sense

I

Philosophy vs. Ideology

A Page from Philosophy 101

William Shakespeare was not only a great poet and playwright; he was also an astute psychologist and a perspicacious philosopher. His philosophy is necessary for his poems and plays to reflect reality. One example, from *Romeo and Juliet*, shows how his philosophy is used to buttress a dramatic point: "That which we call a rose, by any other name would smell as sweet." Here, Shakespeare is calling attention to the difference between the order of being and the order of naming, and how the former takes precedence over the latter. If Romeo had a different surname, he would remain the same person. Juliet is in love with the person who is Romeo and not his name.

In the context of the play, this point is not in the least contentious. In life, however, it is often a source of confusion. A critical point in the abortion debate is how we should think of the human fetus. Do we think of this entity in terms of its *being* and think of it as a human being? Or do we think of the same entity is a blob of tissue, a parasite, a pre-embryo, and other names that disregard what this entity is in its *being*?

To honor the primacy of the order of being requires a certain humility inasmuch as we need to do justice to that being and refrain from imposing our will on it. The order of naming should be, as much as is possible, congruent with the order of being. This is an irrefutable philosophical point, one that should be taught in any Philosophy 101 course. The rose, including its agreeable scent, comes first. It remains a rose whether we name it *rosa* in Italian, *roos* in Estonian, *illipanda* in Swahili, *whakatika* in Maori, or *irozi* in Zulu. Its being does not change no matter how it is named. Its being persists.

Another problem that has become controversial involves gender. Is a human being unalterably male or female? Or is it whatever we call it. Abraham Lincoln once asked an audience how many legs does a dog have if you count his tail as a leg. When people in the audience answered 'five,' Lincoln told them that the correct answer is four. The fact that you called the tail a leg, he explained, did not make it a leg. Lincoln was tutoring his audience in fundamental philosophy.

A Page from Philosophy 101

Baseball great Lou Gehrig died of "Lou Gehrig's Disease." Had his parents Christened him Heinrich, he would have died of the same disease though it would be given a different name – Heinrich Gehrig's disease.

Walker Percy, a fine novelist, was intrigued by the difference between the order of being and the order of naming. In his book *Signposts in a Strange Land,* he calls attention to the difference between the *biological* and the *ontological*. What we want to know about something is what it *is*. Our naming may or may not serve this purpose. If I see a strange bird and ask my bird-watching expert what it is, he may say that it is a "blue-gray gnatcatcher." This name tells me something *about* the bird but does not tell me what it *is*. If he tells me that it is a starling, as Percy, states, "I am satisfied." This particular naming, for Percy, refers to the bird in its being, for me and for everyone else ("We are co-celebrants of being"). At the same time, the name *starling* does not tell me exactly what the bird is, but it does point in that direction.

A young boy comes home with tears in his eyes because of the rude things his peers called him. His mother tries to assuage him by explaining that "sticks and stones may break my bones, but names will never hurt me." Her words may or not be comforting because naming threatens to take the place of being. Her son may not be ready to draw solace from philosophy, but he nevertheless finds some comfort in his mother's words.

Is it possible to name God in such a way that it manifests his being? The theological wisdom of the Middle Ages informs us that "God is known as unknown." The most appropriate name we can apply to God is that "He is the Being who Is." God is the being "whose essence is to be." Existence, however, is not a concept. Hence, it exceeds our grasp. We can grasp an essence: a man, a tree, a dog—but existence eludes us. We know that things exist, but can we apprehend existence in its reality? God exists beyond our capability of naming. To think of God as a father, for example, does not reveal Him in his essence. We know that God is good, true, beautiful, and so on, but not in the way we possess these qualities. As the scholastic philosophers have stated, our knowledge of God is expressed in the negative and analogically. We know what God is not, but not what God is like.

Scripture tells us that our real names are written in the Book of Life. In this case, the order of naming and the order of being perfectly coincide. We wander through life not knowing exactly who we are. But we, as well as our fate, are known to God. In Revelation 20:15, we read as follows: "If anyone's name was not found written in the book of life, he was thrown into the lake of fire. This is what will happen to those who are outside of Christ, whose names are not found written in the Book of life." The meaning of our life on earth is to become who we really are, to live in accordance with our real name.

The Burden of Being Rational

Man is a rational animal. This is the classic definition of the human being who is endowed with a power that distinguishes him from animals. This definition, however, does not imply that man always acts rationally, but he could not act irrationally if he did not possess the capacity to act rationally. He could not deviate from something that he did not have.

Being rational means that one has the ability to reason. This is, of course, an ability that is not always put into practice. Man is complex. His ability to reason is intimately related to his freedom of choice. Therefore, he can make choices that are unreasonable. Reason is a faculty of his being. Being unreasonable requires digressing from his being. The faculty and its misuse are not identical, nor is being unreasonable primary.

Reason is not a burden but a blessing. It is the ability that can be of great practical utility. If I have an important interview in the morning, my reason tells me that I should get a good night's sleep. It also tells me that I must be respectful toward the interviewer throughout the interview. I may not heed the voice of reason and spend the night watching the late, late shows on television and acting in a haughty manner during the interview. Reason, then, is our ally, and has the function of leading us along the right path. It is a blessing and not a burden. Furthermore, our use of reason, which is an abstract faculty, is natural, prompt, and painless.

If reason can be misused, it can also be misunderstood. What reason is certainly not, is something alien to our nature. Being rational is an essential part of our being and, as such, is expressed freely and in the interest of what is good for us. Yet, there are some who believe that people must strain in order to use this natural endowment.

A 2023 survey of pro-abortion unmarried Americans indicates that they are having less sex since *Rose v. Wade* was overturned. According to this long-running survey by Match Group, 87% of those interviewed said that *Roe's* being overturned "has impacted their dating and sex life," with 15% of active daters agreeing that they are now "afraid of getting pregnant or getting someone else pregnant," and

14% saying that they have "less casual sex now and/less sex overall." 54% reported not having sex in the past twelve months, and many have discussed abortion and contraception earlier in their relationship.

The survey provides evidence that more American singles are using reason in making decisions about sex. Now that abortion is no longer regarded as a constitutional right and, as a result, has lost an important degree of authority, the connection between sex and an unwanted pregnancy becomes more obvious. This greater utilization of reason should be commended. Being reasonable is consistent with being human. Nonetheless, this heightened use of reason has been severely criticized.

Justin Garcia, the Kinsey Institute executive director and Match Group adviser, viewed this increased use of reason as being "traumatic." He argues that making more thoughtful and rational decisions has an adverse impact on singles. "It's really remarkable," he states, "that legislation is making people feel more nervous or worried or less comfortable with their sex lives."

Making more thoughtful and reasonable decisions is hardly traumatic or nervousness-inducing. It should be perfectly natural since man is a rational being and natural acts are consonant with his being. Garcia seems committed to both sexual licence and abortion. Therefore, even the use of reason is abhorrent to him because it might rob singles of a certain amount of pleasure. His frame of mind is a clear illustration of how deeply imbedded the abortion mentality is in America. Garcia is more worried about the use of reason than the misuse of sex.

Putting reason into practice is neither burdensome nor difficult. What may be a little difficult for some singles is giving up the pleasure of sex. The opposition to being pro-life has now extended to being opposed to the use of reason. It is misanthropic to denounce reason, especially in a world where the application of reason has brought about great improvements in medicine, travel, housing, agriculture, communications, food processing, and automobile safety. Arguing against reason is obviously self-defeating.

Pope Saint John Paul II states in his Apostolic Constitution *Ex Corde Ecclesiae* (From the Heart of the Church) that "a Catholic University must have the courage to speak uncomfortable truths which do not please public opinion, but which are necessary to safeguard the authentic good of society."

The "uncomfortable truth" is that abortion ends the life of a human being. Would that this truth could be an essential part of education. Truths, however, can fall like dominoes. Denying the truth of the unborn leads to denying the morality of sexual intercourse and ultimately to the denial of the practicality of reason itself.

Al Gore showed his movie about climate change, *An Inconvenient Truth,* with great success (though he was not really dealing with truth). One of his most quoted lines is "What gets us into trouble is not what you don't know, but what you think you know that just ain't so." This sentence could have been better applied to the abortion issue where so many presume that sex is essentially about pleasure, and abortion is simply a choice.

The denunciation of reason may be the final argument in the pro-abortion armament. It may be a turning point because, in this instance, all human beings are now under attack.

The Relevance of St. Thomas Aquinas in Today's World

In the Preface to the 1958 edition of *St. Thomas Aquinas,* Jacques Maritain states that his presentation is not of a *medieval* Thomism, but of a lasting and *present* Thomism." Such a presentation, however, goes against the grain of today's intellectual climate in which progress, and all that it implies, is taken for granted. Can ideas have lasting power? Can something that was said in the 13th century be relevant in the year 2024?

Built-in obsolescence belongs to the world of technology but not to the world of art. John Keats recognized the durability of art when he declared that "A thing of beauty is a joy forever." The works of Plato and Aristotle, Bach and Beethoven, Da Vinci and Michelangelo, Shakespeare and Dante have retained their eternal freshness. Whatever is up-to-date is quickly out-of-date. But it is the glory of the human mind that it can create forms that intimate the eternal. "I am not trying to include the past in the present," Maritain writes, "but to maintain in the *now* the presence of the eternal."

Thomism holds that we should employ reason in order to distinguish the true from the false. By contrast, it is quite common in the modern world to award this important function to popularity, opinion polls, or practicality. Reason, therefore, in the search of truth, is a value that is currently either ignored or rejected. Like Pontius Pilate, contemporary skeptics ask, "What is Truth?" Maritain disdains to place the wisdom of St. Thomas on a political spectrum: "Thomism is neither of the right nor of the left; it is not situated in space, but in the spirit." It is the truth that will make us free.

At the hearing on the case for the canonization of Saint Thomas (August 8, 1319), Friar Giacomo di Viterbo, Archbishop of Naples, believed that God had dispatched three doctors to illuminate the world and the universal Church, "first the apostle Paul, then Augustine, and finally Friar Thomas whom no one would surpass till the end of the world." This, of course, is viewing St. Thomas from on high. But it must be remembered that Aquinas' philosophy is essentially built from the ground up. For the Angelic Doctor, all knowledge begins in the senses. His philosophy, therefore, accords with common sense which places all human beings at the doorstep of philosophy.

G. K. Chesterton stresses, in his remarkable book *St. Thomas Aquinas*, that "Aquinas is almost always on the side of simplicity, and supports the ordinary man's acceptance of ordinary truisms." Aquinas is confident that the ordinary man can grasp the external object and does not remain in a quandary about whether what he sees is real or not real. In this light shines the basis for democracy and the notion that all men are equal. Aquinas invites everyone to the banquet of wisdom and makes no distinction between the master and the "man in the street."

Because ordinary human beings know that they are living in a real world, one which they did not create, they can appreciate the reality of the natural law. And it is this natural law that serves as the basis of morality. Therefore, morality is not arbitrary or relativistic, but solidly anchored in the natural law.

If people find philosophy to be difficult, it may be that they find something else equally difficult, namely humility. For Aquinas, "the virtue of humility consists in this, that one keep himself within his own limits; he does not stretch himself to what is above him." The philosopher begins with humility. He has no interest in dazzling the world with novel ideas. Novelty holds no interest for him. He wants to know something about reality and does not want his ego to get in the way. Aquinas could not have been either a saint or a great thinker if it were not for his profound sense of humility. To see things as they are and not the way I would prefer them to be is the mark of a humble philosopher.

For Maritain, "St. Thomas is properly and before everything else, *the apostle of the intelligence*: this being the first reason why we must regard him as *the apostle of modern times.* Intelligence is not confined to an era. It is the birthright of every person who has ever come into the world. Yet, in the modern world, intelligence is compromised, politicized, or subordinated to power. Intelligence in its purity, nonetheless, is a most reliable witness to truth.

The present age is not philosophical. There are, however, substitutes for philosophy that pretend to be philosophical. In this regard we find popular writers and thinkers who attempt to provide solutions for our therapeutic society. Dr. Ruth, Dr. Laura, and Dr. Phil have had their hour on the stage of philosophy in an attempt to help people who are struggling with day-to-day problems. Worthy as their aims may be, they do not deal with transcendent issues relating to God and the ultimate meaning of life. They seek therapies, but not wisdom.

St. Thomas is a philosopher in the broadest sense, dealing with everything that stimulates the mind and exercises the intelligence. His degree of sanctity and humility are rare. His mind was encyclopedic, having read and digested whatever in the intellectual world of his time was available to him. Moreover, he has been baptized by a number of popes as the Catholic Church's pre-eminent thinker. His feast day is January 24, which is an annual occasion for remembering his importance to everyone who seeks wisdom.

A Sextet of Great Ideas

My last class before the dreaded final exam was usually devoted to a summary of the course and an opportunity for students to ask questions. On one such occasion, a student implored me to give her a list of all the bad ideas. Such a list would be more than encyclopedic. No one has ever catalogued all the bad idea that have come into the world. In fact, new ones are arriving with each passing day.

"It is always simple to fall;" as G. K. Chesterton reminds us, "there are an infinity of angles at which one falls, only one at which one stands." Rectitude, both physically and morally, is the destiny of *Home erectus*.

I did not want to disappoint my eager student. Therefore, I decided to cut her study time immeasurably by informing her that if we have but six great ideas, we are doing quite well. Six is said to be a "perfect" number since it is the sum of all its divisors: 1, 2, and 3. The ancient Pythagoreans were fascinated by the number 6, more for its mystical than for its mathematical significance. Perfect numbers are rare, as is sainthood, and for that reason have a certain nobility. The ancient Greeks correctly calculated the first four perfect numbers as 6, 28, 496, and 8,128.

Mortimer Adler, whom we may call "The Dean of American Philosophers," wrote a book entitled *Six Great Ideas*. It was based on a seminar he conducted at the Aspen Institute in Colorado in the year 1981. The attendees were leaders from the worlds of business, literature, education, and the arts. The sextet of these great ideas consisted of Truth, Goodness, Beauty, Liberty, Equality, and Justice.

The first triad are ideas we judge by, the latter three are ideas we act on. We need the first three to provide a basis for exercising the second three. And here is today's problem in a nutshell. While the secular world is enamored with Liberty, Equity, and Justice, they routinely reject Truth, Goodness, and Beauty. In effect, however, by rejecting the first three, they disable the three that follow.

The year 1981, from a cultural point of view, seems part of a distant past when people held radically different philosophies. During that time to the present, the idea of Truth has undergone a bludgeoning. Today, if one quotes a certain passage from the

Bible, once believed to convey truths, he risks severe penalties. In a moral climate where no one is to be offended, Truth has become a form of "hate speech.' Even in professional circles, truth has been supplanted by scepticism.

The prestigious medical journal *The New England Journal of Medicine* published an article entitled "Pro-life Perinatology – Paradox or Possibility." The authors argue that only the moral sceptic should have a place in prenatal care: "If a physician cannot discuss issues of antenatal diagnosis with patients and present both viewpoints [abortion or birth], then it would be better for all concerned if he or she entered another field. Patients should not be subjected to one-sided arguments for or against antenatal diagnosis and the subsequent options."

Truth, however, stands alone. It does not have equal status with untruth. Withholding truth does not serve the patient well. To say that abortion is the willful killing of a human being, no matter how small, is a truth, though one that may be disagreeable to some people. But it is the Truth that orients us to reality, and not its counterfeit. Scepticism presumes that darkness is not inferior to light. Therefore, Truth is robbed of its status as a Great Idea to allow scepticism to reign.

While Truth may be offensive, Goodness appears to be either too ambiguous or too subjective to have any credibility. At the same time, in common discourse, we speak of the Common Good, a good movie, a good person. Here is what seems to be an unbridgeable gap between ordinary life and philosophy. What we know instinctively, we lose upon reflection. Something is good if it contains or presents all that it should be. We know what a good coffee is and admire another for being such a good person.

The notion of Beauty suffers from the same problem. We know about a beautiful sunrise, a beautiful face, and a beautiful poem. We speak of these as beautiful without hesitation. And yet, when we reflect on the matter, we conclude that beauty is in the eye of the beholder. Beauty, then is no longer a Great Idea, but a private opinion. Philosophers lose the right to say that "Beauty will save the world." DaVinci is just another painter.

Unfortunately, the three popular virtues, Liberty, Equality, and Justice, words that campaigning politicians cannot do without, are unable to operate if they are severed from Truth, Goodness, and Beauty. Liberty would be pointless if it were not harnessed to Goodness. Equality would be unfair to things that distinguished themselves by their Beauty. And Justice could not be attained unless it were based on Truth.

By dismissing the initial triad of Great Ideas, we cripple the second. The six great ideas work together. They are not only Great, but cooperative. They must be honored as an integrated group. If we fervently desire Liberty, Equality and Justice, we must desire with equal fervor, Truth, Goodness, and Beauty.

A Note on the Supreme Wisdom

Wisdom is not only difficult to achieve, but difficult to express. Undertaking the latter, however, is worthwhile since it may serve as a stepping stone to its achievement.

We begin with a notion that is easy to apprehend. There are two fundamental things we can say about anything that exists. First of all, that it is something: a human being, a dog, a tree, or a flower. Philosophers use the word *essence* to refer to all these things that exist. Essence answers the question, "What is it?" A human being has the essence of a human being, a dog, the essence of a dog, and so on. The second thing we can say about anything that exists is that it *exists*. That is, it stands outside of nothingness. All the things in the universe have both an *essence* and an *existence*. These two fundamental features are combined together to give reality to any particular kind of thing. We are all essences who exist.

While it is easy to understand the notion of *essence*, the notion of *existence* eludes us. Although every being is composed of an essence and an existence, the latter is shrouded in mystery. This is because *existence* does not exist. Now, that is a startling statement! The truth of the matter is that we cannot have a concept of existence. We cannot draw a picture of *existence*, though we know without any doubt that it is real. Trying to think of existence all by itself is akin to trying to hear the sound of one hand clapping.

Science is the study of essences. It studies everything from atoms to galaxies, from the one-celled protozoan to the multi-trillion-celled human being. But it cannot turn its attention to *existence*. Once it isolates existence from essence, it becomes tongue-tied. It cannot explain why any particular essence came to be or why it exists at all. It is left to philosophy and theology to deal with the mystery of *existence*.

The distinguished astronomer, Sir Arthur Eddington, was the first to confirm Einstein's "Theory of Relativity." He has complained, however, "that philosophers do nothing to make clear to 'laymen' what the word 'existence' means." The reason for this is the fact that the concept of existence surpasses our capacity to understand, let alone make clear. It is something both real and unintelligible. Gottfried Leibniz's enduring question, "Why is there something rather than nothing?" cannot be answered by scientists for it involves existence which is shrouded in mystery.

It is in the Old Testament that we find the first reference to existence itself, separated from essence. Moses did not know the name of God, but he knew that the Jews would ask him for it. In speaking to God he said, "Lo, I shall go to the children of Israel, and say to them: The God of your fathers hath sent me to you. If they should say to me: what is His name? What should I say to them? And God said to Moses: I AM WHO AM: "Thus shalt thou say to the children of Israel: HE WHO IS, hath sent me to you."

God, therefore, is the "being who is." God's essence, unlike any other essence, is *to be.* And since His essence is to be, He must be eternal. This is an epoch-making statement concerning God and how He is distinct from all His creation in an absolute way. Furthermore, it is because God's existence contributes to that of our own, according to St. Thomas Aquinas, that "all knowing beings implicitly know

God in any and every thing that they know." We are united to God—existence to existence—and that is why we have, in some obscure way, an innate sense of His Being. Since no one can account for his own existence, all things point to the fact that there must be a point where essence and existence coincide. And this point is the being WHO IS.

This theologically based notion of God preceded its philosophical correlative expressed in great detail by St. Thomas Aquinas. As a consequence, a harmony exists between theology and philosophy, faith and reason, nature and grace. As Etienne Gilson states in his book, *God and Philosophy*, "He who is the God of the philosophers is HE WHO IS, the God of Abraham, of Isaac, and of Jacob."

Here is the supreme wisdom: to know that God exists, but not knowing His essence, or how we can imagine Him. Accordingly, Gilson states, in his book *The Spirit of Thomism*, "To understand this supreme truth is to know that we do not know what God is; and to know that, is also to reach the summit of human knowledge in this life."

To think of God as the being Who Is represents the summit of human wisdom. It combines an affirmation of man's philosophical powers with the humility to know God as unknown.

And now, dear reader, I present to you in a single sentence drawn from Jacques Maritain's book *Existence and the Existent* a challenge to your philosophical ability and a precise summary of everything stated above: "Why should it be astonishing that at the summit of all beings, at the point where everything is carried to pure transcendent act, the intelligibility of essence should fuse in an absolute identity with the super-intelligibility of existence, both infinitely overflowing what is designated here below by their concepts, in the incomprehensible unity of *Him Who is*?"

II

Hope vs. Despair

Conservatives, Take Heart

Who is the greatest of all composers? This is not a particularly difficult question to answer. The consensus among musicians, music lovers, and musicologists is Johann Sebastian Bach, who was born in 1685 and died in the year 1750. Richard Wagner hailed him as "The most stupendous miracle in all music." For Robert Schumann, "Music owes as much to Bach as religion to its founder."

It may be surprising to know that this giant of music was more or less forgotten, along with his music, soon after his death. The engraving plates of *The Art of the Fugue* went as scrap metal. Some of his manuscripts were used as wrapping paper by Leipzig butchers and other merchants. His stature as a composer was eclipsed by two of his own sons Johann Christian and Karl Philipp Emanuel Bach. How did this monumental misunderstanding come about?

Johann Sebastian came at the end of an era in musical history when polyphony reigned. As the word denotes, polyphony deployed several melodies at the same time, each of equal importance. The new era introduced homophony in which a single melody predominated. Thus, papa Bach was regarded by many of his contemporaries as old hat, stuffy, and too conservative. His successors in the music world believed that his compositions were a thing of the past.

For approximately 75 years after his death, little of Bach's music was published or performed. Then, a young man of extraordinary musical perception, named Felix Mendelssohn, re-discovered the works of Bach in the Leipzig library. Under the baton of this twelve-year-old prodigy, *The Passion According to St. Matthew* was performed. The rest, as they say, is history.

It is to the everlasting credit of Mendelssohn that he viewed Bach's compositions not according to political categories, but in terms of their sublime beauty. For him, "conservative" or "old-fashioned" were not relevant.

It is a human tendency to over-value what is new and downplay what came before. Soon after, Vatican II libraries were discarding all books published before 1960. Becoming "up-do-date" became a key word that served as a kind of carrying card for those who thought of themselves as progressive. The treasure that the Church held was ignored for what was regarded as new, bold, progressive, and liberal. Conservatives, like Bach in the years after his passing, were disdained. As Joseph Cardinal Ratzinger pointed out in his book *Principles of Catholic Theology: Building Stones for a Fundamental Theology* (1987), "labeling a person conservative is practically synonymous with social excommunication, for it means, in today's language, that such a one is opposed to progress, closed to what is new and, consequently, a defender of the old, the obscure, the enslaving; that he is an enemy of the salvation that change is expected to bring about."

Ratzinger uses the word "salvation" advisedly, for being "progressive" (or liberal, or left-wing) is to be a member of a veritable religion. And this new religion clashes with Catholicism, dividing its members into ambiguous and confusing categories. Moreover, tradition, so basic to any true religion, is scorned or abandoned. The past becomes *passé*. This division of the past from the future is equivalent to giving preference to "what is not" from "what is." The future is "not yet," and its value is yet to be determined.

President Obama wanted to silence all conservative radio talk show hosts. President Biden wanted news delivered to young people to have an exclusively liberal slant. The essential importance of truth is neglected. Jacques Maritain, in *The Peasant of the Garonne*, is uncharacteristically blunt in describing discourse without truth as "bullheaded nonsense."

Being "conservative" does not imply rejecting worthwhile change (consider the popularity a few years ago of Bach played on a Moog synthesizer). While liberals oppose conservatism, they enthusiastically endorse conservationism. The abortion issue, which should unite conservatives and liberals, actually separates them into incommunicable opponents. Being liberal means defending and protecting the lives of whales, snail darters, mud turtles, and all animals on the endangered species list. However, aborting the human unborn is at the top of their agenda. Liberalism in today's world is a poorly-concocted program that is more a temperament than a coherent political strategy. Yet, it prevails because it rides the currents of progressivism and promises a bright future.

Politics owes its popularity to the fact that it appeals to people who do not want to think. Philosophy demands not only thought, but time-consuming thought. Why employ reason when a well-crafted slogan yields immediate practical results?

Isaac Asimov had something worthwhile to say apart from his panoply of science fiction books. Concerning the lack of thought that is commonly found in political discussions, he states as follows: "There is a cult of ignorance in the United States, and there has always been. The strain of anti-intellectualism has been a constant thread winding its way through our political and cultural life, nurtured by the false notion that democracy means that my ignorance is just as good as your knowledge."

Shoddy political categories pose the danger of our missing out on ideas that are truly important. We can thank Felix Mendelssohn for rescuing Bach from oblivion and allowing his music to enter the hearts of minds of untold millions of listeners. He was able to do this because he was primarily concerned with beauty and not fashion. He was neither liberal nor conservative. He was perceptive, an ability that is often lost in contemporary political palaver.

How Thanksgiving Can Conquer Envy

Envy is sorrow at another's good fortune and is properly listed among the Seven Deadly Sins. It makes a person sad and gets him nowhere. It is, therefore, a paragon of futility. Moreover, envy is the hopeless desire to exchange places with the person one envies. Therefore, it is also a rejection of one's self.

A compilation of the thoughts of Saint Josemaria Escriva is contained in a volume entitled *The Way*. Here, the author counsels us to lift our hearts to God, "in acts of thanksgiving many times a day." One reason for doing this is "because he made that man eloquent and you he left tongue-tied."

It is good to be tongue-tied in the presence of a person whom God has richly blessed. We should have joy, not envy, at one who has gifts in greater abundance than the ones that God has bestowed on us. We can be grateful for what God has given us while, at the same time, rejoicing at the gifts he has given others. In this way, thanksgiving can conquer the fruitless vice of envy.

When we are tongue-tied, it is because we cannot find the words that can convey our admiration for another person's talents. We experience the salutary virtue of humility which places us on the right Way on the road to our salvation.

I had this feeling many years ago when I met Leonid Hambro who, in the year 2006, at 86 years of age, returned to the Author of his prodigious gifts. He was a highly regarded concert pianist who performed with the orchestras of Boston, Philadelphia, Chicago, London, and many others. He was also a skilled chamber musician who collaborated with the likes of Jascha Heifetz, Isaac Stern, Fritz Kreisler, and Leonard Rose. He toured worldwide and made more than 100 recordings. He possessed a remarkable ability to sight read. His musical memory was truly prodigious. Upon occasion, he gave "Command Performances" in which he would hand his audience a list of 100 piano works and ask members to choose the program.

Leonid Hambro may be best known, however, for his ten-year collaboration with piano-comedian

Victor Borge. He assumed the role of a "straight man," though, as Howard Taubman, a music critic for the *Times,* remarked, Mr. Hambro is "the laughingest straight man you ever saw."

For 17 years, he was the pianist for WQXR, the radio station owned by *The New York Times Company.* In that capacity, he gave live recitals on the air. It was at the radio station where I met him, shook his hand, and was a bit overwhelmed by his friendly and unassuming air. I was in the presence of a musical giant. Yet, he was genuinely interested in meeting me and being engaged in an amiable conversation.

Thank God for Leonid Hambro. I could not envy him. That would be the wrong response to his graciousness. I was pleased that he was so divinely gifted and possessed talents that I could only dream about. Mr. Leonid Hambro is a gift to the world. I would not mar that gift by responding with any trace of envy.

I was fortunate enough to enjoy similar experiences with other highly gifted pianists such as Eugene Indyic, Alexander Borovsky, Angela Cheng, and Raffi Armenian. God doles out His gifts as He sees fit. Envy is complaining about the Divine prerogative. At the same time, it behooves us to be thankful for the gifts He has given us. We are, indeed, richer than we think. And a debt of gratitude belongs to Saint Josemaria Escriva.

If not Catholicism, then What?

We were not made to get through life by ourselves. We need something outside of ourselves that steers us away from the rocks of despair, on the one hand, and the vanity of egoism, on the other. We are complex beings and need an array of safeguards because there is a multitude of ways in which we can fall. An enemy awaits for every need we have. If we believe only in ourselves, we fall into the abyss of pride; if we believe only in others, we are untrue to ourselves. If we dedicate ourselves only to work, we forfeit the benefits of play; if we dedicate ourselves only to play, we lose sight of life's meaning. We need a great deal of antidotes so that we do not fall. We must find an equilibrium that protects us from tumbling into the trap of one-sidedness.

In the Catholic Church, we find a paragon of balance. In this regard She has no peer. Sin is expiated by forgiveness. Chastisement is tempered by mercy. Nature is elevated by grace. Sexuality is made meaningful by responsibility. Rights are counterbalanced with duties; work is crowned by prayer. Will is tethered to reason. Where there are difficulties, there is hope. Where there is doubt, there is faith. Where there is goodness, there is love. Problems are resolved; order is maintained. No other organization offers such a system of balance.

G. K. Chesterton described this equilibrium in peerless prose when, in his *Orthodoxy*, he summed up the undeviating history of the Catholic Church: "It is always simple to fall; there are an infinity of angles at which one falls, only one at which one stands. To have fallen into any one of the fads from Gnosticism to Christian Science would indeed have been obvious and tame. But to have avoided them all has been one whirling adventure; and in my vision the heavenly chariot flies thundering through the ages, the dull heresies sprawling and prostrate, the wild truth reeling but erect."

The Church must be doing something right since it is the only institution that has survived for as many as 2,000 years. And She has won loyal adherents throughout the world. The Church certainly has both longevity and ubiquity on Her side.

What are the various needs of the human being that give meaning to his life? Apart from the material needs which the secular world provides, there are his spiritual needs. He needs to love and be loved. He needs a sense of purpose. He needs encouragement when he slips, correction when he errs. He needs to be in touch with the Divinity. He needs to be assured that life is worth living and that death is not the final chapter of his life's tenure.

His mind must find truth; his will must discover the good. Beauty in art will enrich his soul, philosophy will lead him to wisdom, and theology will teach him about God. The Catholic Church is the only organization that can satisfy all the needs.

The Church answers all man's spiritual needs, but in a way that forms a synthesis. The Church not only responds to each need, but, collectively, Her responses produce a unified whole. In this sense, the Church is ecological, balancing all the parts into a splendid unicity. There is no need for an admixture from some alien source.

"All being is nuptial," declared the distinguished psychiatrist, Karl Stern. By that he means that every being is mysteriously linked to its complement. Man and woman, Christ and His Church, God and creation, marriage and offspring, and heaven and earth are just a few examples of this nuptial quality. So, too, the individual is a *person,* which is to say, both a unique individual and a caring member of the community.

G. K. Chesterton recounts a conversation he had with a publisher. "That man will get on," said the publisher, "he believes in himself." Chesterton's retort may have stunned and surprised his companion. "The men who really believe in themselves," said the author of *Orthodoxy*, "are all in lunatic asylums." "Well," answered the publisher, "if a man is not to believe in himself, in what is he to believe?" Then, further surprising his friend, Chesterton said, "I will go home and write a book in answer to that question." The book, of course, is *Orthodoxy* and the answer is God and the Church.

If people who believe in themselves are not in lunatic asylums, they maybe campaigning for political office, or writing TV comedies, or providing the world with a novel philosophy that is totally unrelated to reality. Or they may be vandalizing Catholic

If Not Catholicism, Then What?

Churches. Catholicism, on the other hand, because of its balance and wholeness is a recipe for sanity.

If we may refer to the inimitable G. K. once more, let us cite his work *The Well and the Shallows*: "For that peculiar and diplomatic and tactful art of saying that the Catholicism is true, without suggesting for one moment that anti-Catholicism is false, is an art which I am too old a rationalist to learn at my time of life."

We need not be diplomatic to present Catholicism in all its balance and wholeness and invite one to examine it for what it is. One can dispense with any concern for choosing any one of Her rivals. She shines on Her own. There really are no competitors.

The Significance of the Smile

We can learn a great deal about life by observing the reactions of children. A child's smile is an early indication that he is a rational animal. No other animal in the kingdom of animals is capable of smiling. And certainly, hyenas do not laugh.

A child smiles as a way of rejoicing in his discovery of things. His smile is a spontaneous affirmation of the surprising existence of things that he encounters for the first time. It is a wondrous thing for anything to be: a cloud, a flower, a dog, a toy, another person. In his welcoming smile the child is saying, "I'm glad you exist. You surprise me by coming to me out of nowhere!" I greet you with the only gesture I have in my vocabulary—my smile.

As we age and get accustomed to things, we have fewer reasons to smile. We lose our childhood innocence and familiarity takes away what Wordsworth called, "the splendor in the grass and the glory in the flower." But children bequeath to adults an important lesson, that to smile is to affirm someone in his existence. It is a natural way of saying, "I am pleased that you exist." This is the smile that teems with interpersonal significance. In the geometry of human relationships, the smile is the shortest distance between two persons. Comedienne Phyllis Diller, not known for giving geometric advice, states that "a smile is a curve that sets everything straight." Saint Teresa of Calcutta, who spent a lifetime smiling, tells us that, "We shall never know all the good that a simple smile can do."

Charles Dickens paints a most unattractive picture of Ebenezer Scrooge, a man who could not smile: "The cold within him froze his old features, nipped his pointed nose, shriveled his cheek, stiffened his gait, made his eyes red, his thin lips blue, and spoke out shrewdly in his grating voice. A frosty rime was on his head, and on his eyebrows, and his wiry chin. He carried his own low temperature always with him; he iced his office in the dog days; and didn't thaw one degree at Christmas." Scrooge, like the devil, could not smile because his heart had no warmth. Once converted by the magic of Christmas, however, he was a thoroughly changed man: "I am light as a feather, I am as happy as an angel, I am as merry as a schoolboy." At last, he could rejoice in being alive and begin to smile!

The smile is a two-way street. One person smiles because he rejoices in seeing the good in the other; the other smiles back because he delights in the affirmation that a smile bestows upon him. One cannot overestimate the healing significance of the smile. The famed essayist, Joseph Addison has remarked, "What sunshine is to flowers, smiles are to humanity. These are but trifles, to be sure, but scattered along life's pathway, the good they do is inconceivable."

Hal Roach spent his career igniting smiles around the globe. His famous eulogy on the significance of the smile contains these two gems: "It enriches those who receive it without impoverishing those who give; It happens in a flash and the memory of it lasts forever."

The smile is a nonverbal form of communication that goes from heart to heart. It is the key that is preordained to fit anyone else's heart. It is an affirmation of the other's right to be here. It often triggers a smile in return and can even be a prelude to friendship. It is a way of acknowledging both the truth and the goodness of the other.

An infant learns to smile at his mother's breast while the mother re-learns the naturalness of the smile. A community has its basis in the smile. Greeting and farewells are enriched by the smile. Smiles are also conveyors of hope. As long as we can smile, we are on top of things. It is far better to smile than to sulk. It is, as musician, artist, and author Tom Wilson tells us, "A facelift that's within everyone's price range." To quote Mother Teresa once more, "Peace begins with a smile."

A remarkable number of songs are based on the smile. One that is familiar to many contains the words, "Blue skies, smiling at me; nothing but blue skies do I see." It is possible to look at nature and sense that nature is smiling back at you. Theologians might suggest that this is because it is God Himself that is smiling through nature. In this case, the smile represents good things that are about to happen.

The various benefits of smiling are shown in smile therapy. Studies have shown that smiling can improve a person's health by boosting the immune system, lowering the heart rate and blood pressure, reducing pain, and even prolonging life.

Psychologists have also linked regular smiling to better relationships among friends and family. Keep on smiling seems to be good advice, even when, as the song says, "your heart is aching." "That's the time you must keep on trying. Smile, what's the use of crying? You'll find that life is still worthwhile. If you just smile."

Smiles are contagious. The first one is the most important one to start the chain-reaction. Anyone can be the initiator and, as such, swings the door wide open. No credentials are required. Just light up your face with sunshine and put on a happy face.

Lessons from the Garden of Gethsemane

The name, "Gethsemane" (*gath shemani*), meaning "oil press," suggests the presence of an olive grove. It is not unusual for modern trees to grow out of the stumps of old olive trees so that today's olive trees may be rooted in those that were alive during the time of Christ. Over the centuries these trees, because of their association with Christ, have been venerated by Christians and infidels alike. Today, in the Middle East, olive oil is as popular as it was in Biblical times.

It was in the Garden of Gethsemane that several events of great importance took place. In addition, it served as a theater in which intensely dramatic lessons were to be taught. After entering the garden, Jesus told his disciples to remain and pray that they may not enter temptation for the spirit is willing but the flesh is weak. He then took three apostles—Peter, James, and John—with him. Turning to the three, he exclaimed, "My soul is sad, even unto death!" (Matthew 26:38-39). Here, Jesus seemed more vulnerable to his humanity than usual thereby causing the three great distress. Then Jesus cried out, "Abba Father, all things are possible to thee. Remove this cup from me, yet not what I will but what thou willest" (Mark 14:36).

Was this a conflict of two wills? Given His choice by Himself, Christ would have rejected the cup of suffering. But there was a higher, more difficult choice that needed to be made, for the redemption of mankind was at stake. We often find ourselves in a situation that requires the more difficult choice. We may take inspiration during these times from Christ's ordeal in the Garden of Gethsemane. Christ realized that the more difficult choice needed to be made. He could not disobey the will of the Father. He could not spurn the needs of humanity.

The sins of mankind flashed through His mind. "And falling down into an agony he prayed the more earnestly. And his sweat became as drops of blood running down upon the ground." (Luke 22:44). The agony was prolonged and of an intensity that no mere mortal can begin to fathom. Aristotle noted the phenomenon of "hematidrosis" or "bloody sweat."

Lessons from the Garden of Gethsemane

For Christ, however, it was accompanied by extreme agony.

Jesus led his three sleepy witnesses back to where the other eight were sleeping. This time, He was in a different mood: "Sleep on now, and take your rest! It is enough; the hour has come. Behold, the Son of Man is betrayed into the hands of sinners. Rise, let us go. Behold, he who will betray me is at hand." (Matthew 45:46). The betrayer, of course, was Judas accompanied by a large cohort with swords and clubs. They were sent from the chief priests and elders to capture Jesus. "Whomever I kiss," said Judas, "that is he. Lay hold of him."

Peter, in an impetuous act, drew his sword and struck the servant of the high priest, slicing off his right ear. John identifies the victim as Malchus (John 18:10). Jesus healed the man's wounded ear by a simple touch of the hand (Luke 22:51). It would be His final recorded miracle this side of the tomb. Bishop Sheen has commented that as a swordsman, Peter was a good fisherman, suggesting that Peter's aim was to slay the servant. Jesus admonished the apostle who would become the "rock," the Church's first pope, by telling Peter to "put back thy sword into its place, for all those who take the sword will perish by the sword."

In ancient times, the right ear was considered the most important ear, as it was the ear that heard the words of God. In the Bible, the concept of blood on the right served as a visible mark of consecration. Modern science has confirmed that the right ear enjoys an advantage in relation to the processing of verbal stimuli. The fact that Donald Trump's *right* ear was wounded has led to a number of interesting speculations.

"The Pope? And how many divisions has the Pope?" It was madness, in the mind of Joseph Stalin, to think that unarmed followers of the Pope could defeat an armed battalion of soldiers. But, as Christ reminded Peter, He could have summoned more than twelve legions of angels to fight in His behalf. Therefore, the kind of victory Christ had in mind would be achieved not by power but by love. And Peter understood. In the words of Saint John Paul II, "He understood up to his last breath that neither he nor his brothers could fight with the sword; because the kingdom to which he had been called had to be won with the power of love, and with the power of truth, and only in this way."

Indeed, to the practical mind, victory belongs to the most powerful. The message that Christ brings into the world seems unrealistic. Yet history bears out its truth. We are hesitant, even skeptical, because we underestimate the power of love. God is omnipotent. Nonetheless, His motive for creation is love. Power is the instrument through which His love is expressed. And it is through love that Christians flourish. No better example of this can be found than in the fall of the Roman Empire concurrent with the rise of Christianity.

The Garden of Gethsemane teaches the essential lessons of life: the importance of prayer, the need for sacrifice, the redeeming value of suffering, and love for others. If we enter spiritually into that garden, we will never be the same.

III

Tradition vs. Chaos

Abortion and the Golden Rule

While slavery was being hotly contested in 1858, three years before his presidential inauguration, Abraham Lincoln made his most succinct statement against slavery: "As I would not be a slave, so I would not be a master. This expresses my idea of democracy. Whatever differs from this, to the extent of the difference, is not democracy."

This statement, a personal refutation of slavery, has an immediate political significance calling for a political equality which is endemic to democracy. But it also has a moral implication inasmuch as it refers to the Golden Rule, a universally-revered moral principle stating that we should treat others the way would want them to treat us. The Golden Rule can be found in Matthew 7:12 where he writes as follows: "In everything, do unto others what you would have them do unto you." In Luke 6:31, we read, "And as ye would that men should do to you, do ye also to them likewise." If you want to be loved, then love. The Golden Rule is a model of fairness and equality.

By invoking the Golden Rule, Lincoln placed himself on firm grounds. Did Lincoln live and act in accordance with this Rule? A singular incident attests that he did. Frederick Douglass, a former slave, had visited the White House at least three times. On his third visit, he was grabbed and forced out the door by a policeman who believed that since he was black he could not have been invited to the office of the president of the United States. Lincoln saw what was happening and intervened. "Here comes my friend Douglass," Lincoln said to the policeman. He took Douglass by the hand and began chatting with him. Douglass would later reflect on the incident. "In all my interviews with Mr. Lincoln, I was impressed with his entire freedom from popular prejudice against the colored race. He was the first great man I talked with in the United States freely, who in no single instance reminded me of the difference between himself and myself, of the difference of color, and I thought that all the more remarkable because he came from the state where there were black laws."

The Golden Rule, not popularity, is the basis for democracy and it is also the basis for people being just to one another and living together in peace and harmony. Abortion is an egregious violation of the Golden Rule because all the power is invested in one. That "one" has dominion over the unborn who is entirely without power. It is a more complete violation of the Golden Rule than that of slavery since the slave remains alive whereas the unborn is put to death. In other words, there is a stronger reason to oppose abortion than there is to oppose slavery.

Many, however, will argue that the Golden Rule does not apply to abortion because there is no parity between the mother and the being in the womb. Yet the parity is at its purity when one considers that each one of us was, at one time, an unborn child. I can say, therefore, that I am happy that my mother did not abort me. If a mother aborts her child, her action contradicts the action of her own mother. She is saying, as it were, I choose abortion, but I am happy that my mother did not make that same choice.

We were all at one time unborn. As I would not be aborted, so I would not abort. The Golden Rule demand a certain consistency. With regard to abortion, to choose abortion is inconsistent with one's identity. I was once an unborn child, and I am thankful that I was not aborted. In this particular instance,

I am against abortion, though retroactively. But I am being selfish if I am against abortion in one case, where I benefit, but for abortion when it does not affect me directly. Here is an existential clash between what I am against with regard to myself, but for when it pertains to another.

In Leviticus 19:34, we read the following expression of the Golden Rule: "But treat them just as you treat your own citizens. Love foreigners as you love yourselves, because you were foreigners one time in Egypt. I am the Lord your God." We were all foreigners at one time, that time before we migrated from our mother's womb to the outside world. We were all foreigners in this sense. But being a 'foreigner' does not disqualify us from being treated fairly and justly.

The Golden Rule stands firmly against war. Given the history of warfare both between and within nations, it may be said that the Golden Rule is as rare as it is admirable. Abortion is warfare against the unborn.

Because abortion is a widespread rejection of the Golden Rule, it weakens other areas where the Golden Rule should be applicable. A wife's abortion often weakens the bond between her and her husband. As the Golden Rule loses its prestige in society, a host of other human relationships suffer. The Golden Rule holds society together. When it is violated in one area, such as in abortion, it is violated in other areas, perhaps in the area of economics. In this regard, former president Ronald Reagan has said, "We might come closer to balancing the Budget if all of us lived closer to the Commandments and the Golden Rule."

Back to Square One

We are lost! We are lost in the sense that we do not know where we are going. Thus, we wallow in a state of bewilderment and discontent. We sense that there is an end to our travel, a home that offers us final fulfillment. But we do not know where it is or how to get there.

So, let us go back to square one. Let us open the *Summa Theologica* of St. Thomas Aquinas and read what he says at the very outset of his remarkable compendium of wisdom. The first article asks, "Whether, besides Philosophy, Any further Doctrine Is Required?" The first "Objection" states that, "It seems that, besides philosophical science, we have no need of any further knowledge."

Simply stated, this "objection" captures a problem that has persisted over the past 800 years. We are lost because our scientific reasoning cannot lead us out of the very trap that reason has set for us. Reason is at a loss in dealing with the nature of God, the immortality of the soul, the dignity of human life, the origin of the universe, and the ultimate end of the human being. This is not to depreciate the importance of reason, but just to indicate its limitations. And so, we go 'round in circles, exasperated in our attempt to get from reason what reason does not have to give.

We look to the great scientists for help. But their reasoning powers, though extraordinary in themselves, are of no better service than those of laymen. As Aquinas writes, "the truth about God such as reason could discover, would only be known by a few, and that after a long time, and with the admixture of many errors." The most rationally gifted man in the world may be humbled upon realizing the limits of his rational capacities and his need for divine revelation.

We then read Aquinas's refutation: "It was necessary for man's salvation that there should be a knowledge revealed by God, besides philosophical science built up by human reason." Here, the Angelic doctor is speaking to everyone. The final end, which rescues all of us from being lost, is to be with God in Paradise. This is what is meant by our salvation. And in order to fulfill our destiny, we need God's revealed knowledge that reason alone cannot produce.

Faith in God's revealed truth gives the humblest person a kind of knowledge that is superior to anything that reason can uncover. In his book *Reason and Revelation*, Étienne Gilson remarks that "he who merely believes in the word of God knows more than the greatest philosophers have ever known concerning the only matter of vital importance. We should feel justified in saying that the simplest among Christians has a philosophy of his own, which is the only true philosophy, and whose name is: Revelation."

We have given politics center stage and continue to be frustrated by its inability to provide us with the wisdom we need in order to escape from our predicament. We look to science for answers to our deepest questions but are not satisfied with mere theories. God's Word, which we need most, is what we explore least. Thus, we remain lost in a sea of unanswered opportunities.

Robert Jastrow, an American astronomer and planetary physicist (1925-2008), attests to the limitations of reason in his book *God and the Astronomers*: "For the scientist who has lived by his faith in the power of reason, the story ends like a bad dream. He has scaled the mountains of ignorance, he is about to conquer the highest peak; as he pulls himself over the final rock, he is greeted by a band of theologians who have been sitting there for centuries."

Science does not end as a bad dream, most certainly, but only to those who believe that it is omniscient. Science hands the baton over to theology. The two are agreeable partners. They complement each other. Theology begins where reason comes to an end. Science employs reason as far as it goes. Theology is built on faith.

Christ's words concerning the supreme value of the human soul ring out convincingly when He asks, "For what does it profit a man to gain the whole world and forfeit his soul? For what can a man give in return for his soul?" The soul is immortal. Fame and fortune are fleeting. In the secular world, people think of "getting ahead," going places," and becoming "somebody." But it is salvation that reigns over everything else. We are lost because we have neglected our salvation.

Citizen Kane, one of Hollywood's greatest triumphs, is the story of a man who amassed great wealth, but the sum total of all his possessions, in the end, amounted to a collection of mere trinkets. John

Foster Kane was a man who traded his soul for power and lost both. For Aquinas, 'Three things are necessary for the salvation of man: to know what he ought to believe; to know what he ought to desire; and to know what he ought to do."

The beginning of the *Summa* rescues us from being lost. It reminds us of the essential importance of our salvation. It also reminds us of the limitations of science and the importance of faith. We are all equally in need of Revelation. In the order of salvation, there is no caste system. Square one plants a person's feet on the path to salvation.

An Open Letter to the President of a Catholic University

Since university presidents, in general, welcome feedback, I am pleased to respond to one particular president of a Catholic University with the hope of providing some direction. I do this because of the great potential for good that a Catholic school has not only in education but also in the spiritual formation of its students. And what I glean from this president's message, which may or may not characterize his broad mission, is a clear instance of what Jacques Maritain had described as "kneeling before the world."

In a message to all his constituents, he states that "The importance of Equity, Diversity, and Inclusion (EDI) should be understood as foundational to the life of a Catholic university." We may question whether these values are "foundational." Catholicism has a long history. The term "Catholic" can be traced back to St. Ignatius of Antioch in the year 110 AD. It is unlikely that the Catholic Church functioned for so long without foundational values until recently when the secular world, which is not favorably disposed the Catholicism, provided it the form of "Equity," "Diversity," and "Inclusivity." Would not faith, hope and charity, from an historical and theological point of view, be better candidates for being "foundational"?

Every college and university has an admission acceptance rate. Your school's acceptance rate, as posted, is 53%. This means that 47% of applicants are not included. What, then, does "inclusion" mean? Furthermore, of those 47%, many who would represent "diversity" would also be excluded. Is it consistent with "equity," then, to exclude those who, according to your message, should be included? Your message, then, I am afraid to say, is incoherent.

On a practical level, where attempts have been made to implement equity, diversity, and inclusivity (DEI) there has been backlash and repeated failure. There are many reasons for this. "Inclusion" is undefined. It has no boundary. No one should be left out. Should members of any one of the various terrorist groups be included"? Including conflicting parties breeds chaos. If totalitarians are to be included, diversity is at risk. In the clash between opposing factions, equity would be lost. DEI is a formula for self-destruction.

Defending the life of the unborn is not widely upheld by advocates of DEI, which means that they do not believe what they advertise. Justice for the unborn would include these human beings who are diverse in the sense that they inhabit their mother's womb. Abortion negates all three elements of DEI. Its application is selective and certainly not inclusive.

A recent example of the failure of implementing unbounded inclusivity demonstrates its sheer impracticality. On February 8, 2024, a transgendered male injured 3 female basketball players before halftime in a game between KIPP Academy and Lowell Collegiate. Concerned with the safety of the remaining players, the Lowell coach decided to forfeit the game. Said one female commentator, "A man hitting a woman used to be called domestic abuse. Now it's called brave." A video clip has caused an uproar on social media about trans-females (that is, men) being allowed to compete in girls' sports.

Organizations have spent billions of dollars in an attempt to reduce discrimination by implementing

DEI. In an article published in the *Harvard Business Review*, author Lily Zheng states that "There's a big, poorly kept secret in the Diversity, Equity, and Inclusion (DEI) industry . . . the actual efficacy is lower than many practitioners make it out to be."

Geraldine Cochran, an Assistant Professor in the Department of Physics and Astronomy, states that she wants to trade DEI for "love and understanding." Here she is closer to what the president of a Catholic University should be saying. In an article in *Areo* magazine entitled "Why We Should Reject Diversity and Equity as Values," Kevin Butterhof agrees that "the problem with diversity and equity is that, rather than correct for the injustices, they only reverse their flow. They also replace a superior set of values—with an inferior set." The February 23. 2021, issue of *World Economic Forum* featured an article entitled "Diversity, Equity and Inclusion have Failed". Author Aida Marian Davis concludes that "existing DEI initiatives only expose discriminatory attitudes, but do nothing to mitigate their effects on those who suffer from them." Some critics prefer using the word "belonging" rather than "Inclusivity." No one seems to be altogether happy about implementing DEI. The trio of words are inadequately defined and presuppose a list of virtues they do not represent.

Faith, hope, and love are decidedly practical. Faith gives us a belief in God, hope offers us our ultimate destiny, while love of God and neighbor is faith and hope put into practice. Love is the form of all virtues, faith enlightens us about truth, and hope gives us a reason to keep trying especially in moments of discouragement.

Karol Wojtyla, later Pope Saint John Paul II, had the courage to speak the faith in the face of dangers posed by Nazis and Communists. The dangers of speaking the faith today in North America are far less severe. Retreating into political correctness, the fear of offending someone, not being branded as "conservative," by comparison, are trivial. A president of a Catholic University needs the courage to proclaim the faith and the intelligence to see through the sham that the secular world proposes. It is a great challenge to be in a position of authority at a Catholic institution. To acquiesce to secular trends, especially those that do not work well even in the secular world, is to abandon the challenge. Your predecessor saw fit to fly the rainbow flag which, in my understanding, is to tell the world that this institution, though named otherwise, is anti-Catholic. It is a formal declaration of hypocrisy.

May your experiences bring you wisdom and courage. May you be open to legitimate criticism and firm in your resolve to carry out the sacred duties of being the president of a Catholic University. May God be with you and with all your students. Amen.

An Open Letter to Harrison Butker

On May 11, 2024, Harrison Butker, a kicker for the Kansas City Chiefs, gave a commencement address to the graduates of Benedictine College located in Atchison, Kansas. His presentation was thoroughly Catholic, but the backlash was extreme, some calling for his dismissal. While an editor might have modified some of his phrases and points of emphasis, his presentation did not warrant the unfair criticism it triggered. I have sided and sympathized with Mr. Butker as indicated below.

Bravo!! You have just kicked the equivalent of a 75-yard field goal! Not too much to the left nor too much to the right, but right down the middle. Strength and accuracy, two highly esteemed qualities on display for the world to see, marvel, and appreciate. As Frank Leahy, former football coach of a champion Notre Dame squad used to say, "When the going gets tough, the tough get going." As you are well aware, the Church is going through a tough time, a time that elicits a response from the best of its members. And you answered the bell.

You are right on when you say that feminists have lied to women. Consider this comment from arch-feminist Betty Friedan in her book *The Feminine Mystique*, a veritable instruction manual for housewives that sold over a million copies: "It is not an exaggeration to call the stagnating state of millions of American housewives a sickness. The problem—which is simply the fact that American women are kept from growing to their full human capacities—is taking a far greater toll on the physical and mental health of our country than any known disease."

This statement is more than a lie. It is Mendacity with a capital M! And it is not an exaggeration to say that it is diabolical. And yet, it was well received and widely promoted. A lie, according to a Russian proverb, can get around the world before you can get your boots on. But, as you know only too well, it is the Truth that makes us free.

Another person of insight and vigor, Winston Churchill, said this about the family as a training ground for a better society: "There is no doubt that it is around the family and the home that all the greatest virtues, the most dominating virtues of human society, are created, strengthened, and maintained." And that great lexicographer, Samuel Johnson, stated that "to be happy at home is the ultimate result of all ambition, the end to which every enterprise and labor tends, and of which every desire prompts the prosecution." In the twilight of our lives, we will not look back and say, "I should have spent more time going to committee meetings or selling used cars, or cleaning other people's homes, or working for the Democratic Party." The family is, as Robert Frost once said, somewhat facetiously, "Home is the place where, when you have to go there, they have to take you in." The family is permanent; success is fleeting. Worldly success is not self-generating as is the family that proceeds from marriage to children to grandchildren and down through the corridors of time.

If some of your misunderstood words have won you enemies, that is the inevitable sign that you stood up for something important. You are accustomed to opposition on the gridiron, an opposition that makes victory, when it comes, all the sweeter. Recall the words of St. Paul in 2 Timothy 4-7: "I have fought the good fight. I have refinished the race, and I have kept the faith." With allies like St. Paul, you are in good company. Christ had His enemies and commanded us to love them. Our enemies can make us stronger.

The ironic factor in playing the game of life, to put the matter in football terms, is that even the referees are against us. The Media does not always play fair. But then, again, God is on our side.

Do not let the criticism from the nuns upset you, though I am sure it does not. It is hard to understand how they seemed to have ignored the salient fact that Mary was a housewife. Christ returned to the Father at 33, but only 3 of those years were spent outside the household in public ministry. Mary, the Mother of God, raised the dignity of the housewife to an unparalleled level. As she stated in her Magnificat, "From this day all generations will call me blessed."

God must love housewives as he loves the poor since He made so many of them. Indeed, He loves everyone, but holds a special place for housewives, and housewives who become mothers and grandmothers. The succession of generations far outweighs in importance any series of promotions in the workplace. It is incontestable that worldly success is overrated, while the family, and especially the duties of the housewife, are unjustly maligned.

An Open Letter to Harrison Butker

Your commencement address was intended to reach a relatively small audience, but, as it turned out, you were delivering a message to the whole world, and one that it desperately needs to hear. God provided you with a high-powered amplifier. No other commencement address received nearly as much publicity. The repercussions will no doubt be more positive than negative

May God continue to guide you, for you are on the right path. Prayers and peace to your wife and two daughters. May they be imbued with your faith and your courage.

Phyllis McGinley Revisited

Things have gotten out of hand. John Paul II tirelessly spoke of the complementarity of the sexes, marriage as a sacrament, and how "humanity passes through the family." Today, we have same-sex marriages, DINKS (dual income no kids), easy divorce, and rampant abortion. Domesticity is regarded as a trap, housework is drudgery, and children are a burden.

We have a president who encourages abortion so that women can fulfill their potential, blithely ignoring the fulfilling role motherhood. It is unimaginable that he would discourage women from going into politics so that they could fulfill their other potentials. People would find such a statement unintelligible.

Betty Friedan's book *The Feminine Mystique* (1963) made the case that women had been cornered into the domestic sphere and, as a result, many of them lost their identities. Her book sold over a million copies and was immensely influential. "It is not an exaggeration," Friedan wrote, "to call the stagnating state of millions of American housewives a sickness. The problem—which is simply the fact that American women are kept from growing to their full human capacities—is taking a far greater toll on the physical and mental health of our country than any known disease."

Friedan may have denied that she was not exaggerating, but her conclusions were tantamount to a textbook example of hyperbole, so much so that it warranted a rebuttal. Phyllis McGinley had been praising domesticity for years in such magazines as the *Ladies Home Journal* and *Glamour*. Her publisher, therefore, prodded her to write a rebuttal to all those, who, like Friedan, were deprecating the housewife. The result was *Six Pence in Her Shoes* which remained on the *New York Times* bestseller list for 26 weeks.

In the years that have followed, McGinley's defense of domesticity, brilliant as it is, may have faded, as most books do, into the unremembered past. But it is quality work. McGinley has that fortuitous combination of literary talent and down-to-earth common sense. It justifies being revisited.

The *New York Times* stated that *Six Pence in Her Shoes* "should be a joy and a boon to the down-trodden women of America who are being urged to get out there a land a job." According to the *Boston Globe*, "The rewards of homemaking have seldom had such a warm and wise tribute as Phyllis McGinley gives it . . . executed with love, humor and candor." Finally, the *Baltimore Sun* found it to be "a reward to the women who give their hearts to the most joyous and ancient of professions."

For McGinley, "It is perfectly apparent," she writes, "that ours it not only the oldest profession in the world but the most numerous. It is not the daughters of Joy who are seniors of a calling, but we, the handmaids of the home. . . I am one of an enormous, an antique sisterhood, each of us bent on much the same ends, all of us doing our able or fumbling best to hold the planet steady on its axis by such primitive expedients as hanging window curtains, bandaging knees, or getting meals to the table on time."

There is nothing narrow in her view of domesticity. Her book mirrors her life and discusses in a most amiable way, myths, manners, and moralities, punctuated by guests, books, friends, children, and the "paraphernalia of life." "By temperament I am a nest builder," she proudly admits. "I have other occupations, chiefly writing and the delights of conversation. Yet to keep a house is my native vocation and I consider it an honorable estate." Her Pulitzer Prize was more an incident than an essential.

Her perspective is shared by her husband, Bill Hayden, who says, "I don't think of her as a writer, I think of her as my wife and the mother of my children." First things first, the family comes before everything else. Like Agatha Christie who got some of her best ideas while washing dishes, Phyllis McGinley found herself working on her poetry while cooking dinner.

She has heard all the complaints. Housework is monotonous, frustrating, and never finished. It is drudgery. She does not cite G. K. Chesterton's book, *What's Wrong with the World,* but would have loved to have him as a dinner guest. "If drudgery means only hard work," said the great essayist, "I admit that the woman drudges in the home." But this form of drudgery is not "trifling, colorless and of small import to the soul." Nor is it narrow. "How can it be a large career to tell other people's children about the Rule of Three, and a small career to tell one's own children about the universe?"

In her chapter on "How not to kill your husband," she reminds her readers that "husbands, like babies and other people, thrive on love and wither without it. It is the best life-preserving medicine in existence. But any woman who can't figure that out for herself will never learn it anyhow."

The *New York Times* hailed *Six Pence in Your Shoe* as "the most impressive book of feminine philosophy since Lindbergh's *Gift from the Sea*." McGinley is "feminine" but not a "feminist." For a woman to be feminine is to be herself. To be a feminist is to try to be something other than herself. God loves housewives as he does the poor because he made so many of them. "It is time," she tells the world, "we also learned to love ourselves."

www.ingramcontent.com/pod-product-compliance
Lightning Source LLC
LaVergne TN
LVHW051831080426
835512LV00018B/2810